VIOLENCE IN AMERICA

INQUIRY INTO CRUCIAL AMERICAN PROBLEMS
Series Editor JACK R. FRAENKEL

VIOLENCE IN AMERICA:

What Is the Alternative?

Second Edition

Jack Zevin

Associate Professor of Education
Queens College
New York, N.Y.

PRENTICE-HALL, INC., ENGLEWOOD CLIFFS, N.J.

Photo Credits

Wide World Photos, viii, 14, 21, 35, 48, 61, 64, 67, 86, 96; Culver Pictures, Inc., 4, 7; Christy Park from Monkmeyer Press Photo Service, 13; C. Ursillo from De Wys Inc., 22; Henry Monroe from DPI, 16; © 1970 Burk Uzzli from Magnum Photos, Inc., 29; © Jim Anderson from Woodfin Camp & Associates, 42; Woodfin Camp & Associates, 55; Mimi Forsyth from Monkmeyer Press Photo Service, 81.

Cover designed by Diane Kachalsky.

Library of Congress Cataloging in Publication Data
ZEVIN, JACK,   comp.
    Violence in America.
    (Inquiry into crucial American problems)
    Bibliography: p.
    1. Violence—United States—Addresses, essays,
lectures. 2. United States—Social conditions—1960–
—Addresses, essays, lectures. I. Title.
HN90.V5Z48 1977   301.6'33'0973   76-20601
ISBN 0-13-942326-5
ISBN 0-13-942318-4 pbk.

Printed in the United States of America

10 9 8 7 6 5 4 3 2 1

Prentice-Hall International, Inc.,
London
Prentice-Hall of Australia, Pty. Ltd.,
Sydney
Prentice-Hall of Canada, Ltd.,
Toronto
Prentice-Hall of India Private Ltd.,
New Delhi
Prentice-Hall of Japan, Inc.,
Tokyo

PREFACE

The series INQUIRY INTO CRUCIAL AMERICAN PROBLEMS focuses upon a number of important contemporary social and political issues. Each book presents an in-depth study of a particular problem, selected because of its pressing intrusion into the minds and consciences of most Americans today.

A number of divergent viewpoints, from a wide variety of different *kinds* of sources, encourage discussion and reflection, and help students to realize that the same problem may be viewed from a number of different vantage points. Of major concern throughout is a desire to help students realize that honest individuals may differ in their views.

After a short introductory chapter, Chapter Two presents a brief historical and contemporary background on the central issue. The chapters that follow explore the issue in detail. A conscientious effort has been made to avoid endorsing any one viewpoint as the "right" viewpoint, or to judge the arguments of particular individuals or organizations. Conclusions are not drawn for students. Instead, a variety of positions are presented, along with open-ended questions and involving activities, so that students can arrive at and evaluate their own conclusions.

Great care has been taken to make these books substantive, highly interesting to students, and readable. Whenever possible, dialogues involving or descriptions showing actual people responding and reacting to problematic situations are presented. Briefly, each book

- presents divergent, conflicting views on the issue under consideration;

- gives as many perspectives and dimensions on the issue as space permits;

- presents articles on a variety of reading levels;

- deals with real people involved in situations of concern to them;

- includes questions which encourage thought about and discussion of the various viewpoints expressed;

- includes activities that involve students and lead to further consideration of the problems presented;

- provides cartoons, photographs, and other illustrations to help students arrive at a more complete understanding of the issue under study.

JACK R. FRAENKEL
Series Editor

v

CONTENTS

1
INTRODUCTION

A 22-year-old policeman stops to buy cigarettes. As he walks back to his car in full view of his partner, a man walks up to him and stabs him three times in the neck. He dies a few hours later.

New low-income housing is going up in a middle-class neighborhood. Construction workers who arrive on the job find a large, angry crowd carrying signs indicating their opposition to the project. They block the workers' path to the construction site. Police arrive to open a path for the workers. Scuffles break out between police and protestors. Many people are injured, some arrested.

A wealthy young woman is having dinner with friends in her apartment. Armed, masked intruders break down the door and order everyone to the floor. They kidnap the young woman and hold her for a huge ransom.

Over a warm spring weekend, almost all the windows in a large secondary school are smashed by vandals.

A young man is arrested and imprisoned for armed robbery. He shows signs of being psychologically disturbed. After six months, he hangs himself with a rope made from strips of bed sheets.

Tons and tons of waste are dumped into a lake by a large factory. The lake water is no longer fit to drink from or swim in. Despite legal suits to halt dumping of wastes into the lake, verdicts are overturned by higher courts.

Firemen answer an alarm. When they arrive they are hit with bottles, rocks, and garbage.

Truckers block interstate highways in protest over higher gas and oil prices, wages and taxes. Some teamsters do not go along with these tactics. A few of these find their trucks sabotaged. Several are fired on as they speed along the highway, lose control, and are killed in crashes.

Two youthful gangs meet on an empty lot for a shoot-out. Several boys are killed, many seriously injured.

A drunken driver swerves wildly along a shop-lined street and finally crashes into a telephone pole on the sidewalk. Several bystanders are injured.

A two-year-old knocks a glass off the kitchen table. His parents, in a fit of rage, punish him by forcing his hand over a lighted gas burner. The child is taken to the hospital. A doctor reports the parents to the police and they are arrested.

Every day, every month, every year, one or more incidents like these   **1** occur in every city and town in America. Newspapers, TV, magazines, and other media report such events quite regularly. Some kinds of incidents occur less than others, but they are all very much with us.

Besides happening in the same country, these incidents share a common result: All cause harm and injury to people and/or damage to property. Each is a sample of what we call violence. There is no shortage of examples.

Violence is a negative word. Most people claim to be opposed to it, yet acts of brutality, murder, war, vengeance, and hatred appear regularly. Newspapers and the news on TV appear to concentrate on the reporting of crimes, riots, and brawls. People spend great sums of money to read about, hear, or see real or fictitious acts of violence. Violence on movies and TV is commonplace. Parents often buy their children toy guns or war games, go to see rough sports, or use force in their homes.

Yet, though many of us seem fascinated by conflict and aggression, we also are deeply fearful of something happening to us or to our families. Today, especially, many Americans seem to be afraid. They believe that an unprecedented wave of violence is sweeping the country. Many feel surrounded by dangers, and, as a result, the demand for more police protection, guards, and protective devices grows. So does the demand for the suppression of unpopular protests or abrasive groups. Some citizens resort to violence to keep "undesirable" people out of their home towns or neighborhoods. Other citizens fear the police, who are supposed to protect them, and attempt to drive the police away. Still others fear and distrust both the police and their fellow men. These fears and hatreds often lead to open hostilities. The frequency and regularity of violence in our society sets us to wondering why—why has it all happened?

Many books, reports, and research papers have been written about the numerous areas of violence. Still, we are not completely certain of its causes or of its effects on our minds and hearts. Various types of violence have been catalogued, ranging from the subtly psychological to the brutally physical. Several kinds have been more widely publicized than others. These include conflicts between races, between ethnic groups, and between those with differing political views. Extremists of the right and of the left frequently dislike each other enough to engage in abuses and attacks. Protest activities, although sometimes peaceful, at times lead to riots, police brutality, destruction of property, or psychological harm.

Last but not least, the forces of law and order themselves—the police, the National Guard—often succumb to hatred and disorder. Police officers who feel a violent disgust for lawbreakers, or for the poor, or for those who are abusive sometimes become violent. The police may then attack part of the public they are supposed to serve. Often called pigs while on missions of protection, many police officers are frustrated and confused as to their role. Hostility is present in many parts of the country, and such hatreds and fears are often expressed in words and deeds of violence which vary in intensity as mood and circumstances change.

When a society is in turmoil, still more conflict is encouraged. Mentally sick and disturbed people surface in these times to inflict still greater damage to American life. Their actions feed new fuel to the flames of violence, and spur still greater study of the subject.

Schools of thought, however, are divided on some of the more important issues. Some insist that people have always been violent and will continue to be so; not much can be done about it. Others believe that violence is a social ill brought about by social and historical causes. Still others believe that violence can be good, and feel it has a place in our lives.

A second controversy centers on the degree of violence we are currently experiencing. One school of thought argues that Americans have always been a conflict-ridden people, and that they are no worse today than they have been in the past. A second school states that violence is on the increase, and the wave hasn't peaked yet. A third view holds that Americans have become better off in almost every way, but more fearful of changes and the troubles that go with them. This view believes we are exaggerating our problems. As you read the materials in this book, think about which school of thought seems most supportable.

A number of questions will be considered to help you come to some conclusions about the causes and significance of violence in our society. Some of the more important of these questions are:

1.   What do we mean by violence? What sorts of acts and situations are covered by the term?
2.   Are we more violent today than in the past?
3.   Why do people act in a violent way?
4.   What are the effects of violence?
5.   What alternatives to violence exist?

Each chapter that follows presents data that will help you form your own conclusions about the nature, origin, and effects of violence.

2
ARE WE MORE VIOLENT THAN EVER?

The Battle of Bunker Hill.

From its beginning, American history has been filled with violence. Brutality was commonplace during the epoch that brought migrants from the Old World to the New. The Indian tribes who met the first Europeans had a long tradition of warfare and intertribal hatreds, fighting one another for slaves, hunting grounds, or glory. European settlers came from societies where conflict was also firmly established. Often, it was the victims of religious or political persecution who landed on the North American continent, bringing with them their own religious intolerance and ethnic hatreds. Some settlers had taken part in bloody struggles between Catholics and Protestants, Anglicans and Puritans, or Puritans and Quakers, in which others had been killed or mutilated for their beliefs. Thus the stage was set for a classic confrontation between two culturally different, but violence-prone, peoples.

Europeans and Indians did share some values. They both saw conflict as something glorious, exciting, and even ennobling. Though there were early attempts to work together, Indians and Europeans soon saw that their life styles did not mix well. They often misunderstood, or were hostile, to each others' beliefs. And they discovered that hunting and farming were economic systems that did not easily occupy the same space. As Europeans cleared land for farms and destroyed wildlife, they encroached more and more on Indian lands.

One early conflict was King Philip's War. New England settlers were expanding their farms and landholdings at a rapid rate, pushing the Indians farther and farther into the interior. A shrewd and powerful chief, called King Philip by the English, united most of the tribes of the region. In 1675, when a New England court executed three of his men, war began. The united Indians attacked many towns. Settlers fled to more populated and fortified areas. The raids were carried right up to the outskirts of Boston, but the tide of battle soon turned. Armies were raised in Massachusetts and Connecticut. With more modern weapons and better organization combined against them, King Philip's warriors were eventually killed and scattered. Whole villages were massacred by whites. Finally the chief himself was cornered and shot. This "victory" was commemorated by beheading the chief and exhibiting his bloody head atop Fort Hill Tower in Plymouth. The war's result was devastating. Several tribes were completely destroyed. For others, defeat meant slavery on other tribal lands. Three thousand Indians died in this war.

For the colonists, King Philip's War meant a thousand deaths. It also increased the colonists' great fear and hatred of the Indians, even though the tribes of the region never recovered from the war. The wave of settlement pushed on, and the events of King Philip's War were repeated many times—from New England of 1676 to the last stand of General Custer at the Little Big Horn in 1876.

From Revolutionary War to Civil War

The United States—born in violence! This is a popular image of what really happened during America's early days. The Revolutionary period is filled with numerous examples of ethnic, political, social, and economic conflict. From the beginning, Americans participated in violence against people who held unpopular political views. Tories, supporters of the King of England, were frequently viewed with hatred and suspicion by many colonists, particularly the Revolutionaries. Many were humiliated, beaten, and killed. Others were forced to flee the country. Burning the homes of British sympathizers was common. And as the following quotation shows, mob violence was a regular treatment accorded Tories or neutrals in Revolutionary towns:

In November 1774, David Dunbar of Hallifax aforesaid, being an Ensign in the Militia, a mob headed by some of the Select Men of the Town, demand[ed] his colours[1] of him. He refused, saying, that if his commanding officer demanded them he should obey, otherwise he would not part with them:—upon which they broke into his house by force & dragged him out. They had prepared a sharp rail to set him upon; & in resisting them they seized him (by his private parts) & fixed him upon the rail, & was held on it by his legs & arms, & tossed up with violence & greatly bruised so that he did not recover for some time. They beat him, & after abusing him about two hours he was obliged, in order to save his life, to give up his colours.

A parish clerk of an Episcopal Church at East Haddum in Connecticut, a man of 70 years of age, was taken out of his bed in a cold night, & beat against his hearth by men who held him by his arms & legs. He was then laid across his horse, without his cloaths, & drove to a considerable distance in that naked condition. His nephew Dr. Abner Beebe, a physician, complained of the bad usage of his uncle, & spoke very freely in favor of government; for which he was assaulted by a mob, stripped naked, & hot pitch was poured upon him, which blistered his skin. He was then carried to a hog sty & rubbed over with hog's dung. They threw

6   [1]A flag or banner of a country, regiment, etc.

the hog's dung in his face, & rammed some of it down his throat; & in that condition exposed to a company of women. His house was attacked, his windows broke, when one of his children was sick, & a child of his went into distraction upon this treatment. His gristmill was broke, & persons prevented from grinding at it, & from having any connections with him.[2]

With the consolidation of the United States, relative peace prevailed for a time. However, there were undercurrents of violence. With the expansion of the slave system in the South, reports began to crop up of ugly incidents between masters and their slaves. Slavery itself was degrading, but in addition many slaveholders mistreated their slaves. Often, a slave revolt was the result.

The capture of Nat Turner.

[2]Douglass Adair and John A. Schultz, eds., *Peter Oliver's Origin and Progress of the American Rebellion: A Tory View.* Stanford, Calif.: Stanford University Press, 1961, pp. 155–157.

One of the largest slave revolts was Nat Turner's rebellion. Nat Turner was a slave in Southeastern Virginia, an area of fairly large plantations. He learned how to read and used the Bible to justify his hatred of slavery. Many of his fellow slaves looked to him as a religious leader. In 1831, after what he interpreted as a sign from God, Nat Turner formed a small band of slaves for the purpose of insurrection. They started by killing his master and all of his master's family. Then they went from house to house murdering as they went. After a few days of action, the slaves encountered a band of armed white men. As they were about to defeat this group, militia arrived and the slaves fled into the wilderness. Vigilante committees tracked them down, and a general massacre of black men followed. Turner was finally captured and put to death. Such revolts stirred Southern fears of uprisings, especially where slave populations were large. Cruel and repressive measures were instituted to keep the slaves quiet and well controlled.

Examples of violence were frequent during the events of the Civil War era. Just before the war, pro- and antislavery forces were almost always at each others' throats. In proslavery towns, abolitionists were not allowed to speak, their newspapers were burned, and editors were sometimes killed. Antislavery towns often harassed officials who came searching for fugitive slaves. Slaves were, in fact, often hidden in those towns, but no one would tell where. Particularly in border areas, organizations were formed to keep an eye on and to persecute pro- or antislavery people.

The War itself brought death to hundreds of thousands of soldiers, and to hundreds of thousands of civilians as well. The South was wrecked. General Sherman is notorious for having burned a wide swath of land and property throughout the State of Georgia, including some of its best farmland. Prisoners were often treated as animals—by both sides. The detention camp at Andersonville was infamous for the brutality, both psychological and physical, it inflicted upon the Union prisoners. The camp commander was eventually tried as a war criminal.

After the Civil War

Soon after the war, many whites again attempted to gain control over their recently emancipated slaves. In many communities a secret brotherhood was formed for this purpose. Its white bedsheet costumes and cross-burning tactics made the Ku Klux Klan notorious. A black petition from Kentucky, written in 1868, asking for federal aid, gives an idea of Klan methods and results:

1. A mob visited Harrodsburg in Mercer County to take from jail a man name Robertson, Nov. 14, 1867.
2. Smith attacked and whipped by regulation in Zelun County Nov. 1867.

3. Colored school house burned by incendiaries in Breckinridge Dec. 24, 1867.

4. A Negro Jim Macklin taken from jail in Frankfort and hung by mob January 28, 1868.

5. Sam Davis hung by mob in Harrodsburg May 28, 1868.

6. Wm. Pierce hung by a mob in Christian July 12, 1868.

7. Geo. Roger hung by a mob in Bradsfordsville Martin County July 11, 1868.

8. Colored school Exhibition at Midway attacked by a mob July 31, 1868.

9. Seven persons ordered to leave their homes at Standford, Ky. Aug. 7, 1868.

10. Silas Woodford age sixty badly beaten by disguised mob. Mary Smith Curtis and Margaret Mosby also badly beaten, near Keene Jessemine County Aug. 1868.[3]

By 1871 the influence and membership of the Ku Klux Klan had declined, but in 1915 a new Klan carried its activities into Northern communities as well as Southern ones. Cross-burnings and intimidation were extended to Catholics, Jews, and immigrants of all nationalities. Klan organizations flourished in atmospheres of racial and ethnic hatred.

Meanwhile, with the opening of the West, vigilante groups flourished in frontier areas and in newly founded towns. Places where money was to be made, where communications were poor, and where the law was absent gave rise to groups that took the law into their own hands. Suspected criminals or wrongdoers were often executed on the spot by a lynching, or "necktie party." Many innocent people, as well as those that were guilty, probably died this way.

A tough Vigilance Committee was formed in Montana in 1884. Granville Stuart, a wealthy, educated, and powerful rancher (later state land agent), was its leader. Many of the area's most prominent citizens took part in this group. On grounds that lawlessness prevailed in their county, the vigilantes took the lives of 35 alleged cattle and horse thieves. Not one case went to trial or was ever substantiated with evidence. Stuart was an early American example of do-it-yourself "law and order."

Before and after the 1884 Montana vigilantes, many Americans have been willing to use violence to achieve order. Early San Francisco was ruled by a Vigilance Committee of great fame, and at the present time some neighborhoods of large American cities are patrolled by "citizen's groups" who attempt to supplement police patrols in high-crime areas.

[3]From "Petition to Congress Against Violence," U.S. Senate, 42nd Congress, 1st Session, quoted in Joanne Grant (ed.), *Black Protest.* New York: St. Martin's Press. Copyright © Fawcett Publications, 1968.

While men were taming the West, new industries were springing up all over the country. As industry grew, so did the American labor movement. Economic violence associated with the struggles between management and labor added many another bloody chapter to American history. Laborers often formed secret organizations in places where management was very powerful. Early unions resorted to secret violence and sabotage to pressure management into reforming working conditions or increasing wages. There were hundreds of violent disputes, especially during the late-nineteenth and early twentieth centuries.

Henry Clay Frick, an immensely wealthy industrialist, and head of the Carnegie Steel Corporation, broke with an already recognized union over wage demands in 1892. The union promptly struck the company. Frick decided to thwart the strike rather than settle it. He hired a small army of Pinkerton[4] detectives to take the plant away from the union men. The Pinkerton men were to come up the river on a barge and invade the factory. The plot was discovered, and the strikers met the barge as it landed. A pitched battle broke out. Result: several dead on each side and many wounded. This action was repeated again, with the same result, until the Pinkertons surrendered. Upon giving up, the detectives were rushed by the union men, who beat them with fists, clubs, and iron bars. The National Guard was called up to stop the violence. It, too, encountered violence. Labor leaders were arrested, but juries refused to convict them. The whole town was in turmoil, until Frick hired hundreds of strikebreakers who secretly entered the plant and took the place of the union workers. Thus was a strike broken—a strike that included police, union, and management violence.

Dangerous and violent strikes spread all across the country. The years from the 1880s through the 1930s were full of large-scale examples. Even today disputes occur. A strike against American Telephone and Telegraph in 1971 lasted many weeks. As time went on, and frustrations grew, more and more incidents of harassment of nonunion help were reported. Lines were cut, endangering many vital services such as police and ambulance aid. Threats were made by the company to fire workers, to cease negotiations. Finally, a settlement was reached, and the trouble receded.

As cities and industries have grown, so has organized crime. At many periods of our history, criminals have even been glorified and turned into heroes. Jesse James was a forerunner of the romanticized bandit, the little guy attacking big government, big business, and the forces of control. Especially in hard times, criminals who appeared glamorous and fast-living came into the limelight. Perhaps a crescendo of notoriety was reached in the 1930s by John Dillinger, the bank robber; and by Al Capone, the gang leader. At the height of his power, it was reported that Capone controlled the town of Cicero, Illinois, had forced his own man to be accepted as its Mayor, kept a private army of as many as a thousand men, amassed a fortune of millions, and

[4]A private detective agency.

managed a bootlegging system from Florida to Canada worth $60 million a year.

While few individualists like Capone are left, the "mob," "syndicate," or "Mafia" is still very much with us. Dead bodies found in trunks or floating in rivers are still often linked with a gangland feud. Americans find gangsters exciting copy. They buy millions of books about them.

Racial problems, labor disputes, and criminal activity have all continued to the present time. Even during World War II, when most Americans were directing their concern toward fighting on two fronts, race and ethnic conflict seems to have increased. During the war many blacks found opportunities to work in defense industries which had previously been barred to them. President Roosevelt aided their cause by ordering an end to all discrimination in defense plants. Detroit was a center of defense production, much of it being done by the big automobile companies. Only since 1941 had blacks been taken into the United Automobile Workers Union—the U.A.W. In this setting, a large-scale race riot broke out in Detroit in 1943. The locale was a popular amusement park, the immediate cause a fight between a black man and a white. Rumors began to spread, first about attacks on black women, and then about attacks on white women. After a short time, blacks began to loot and burn stores. Police fired at them. Then whites attacked blacks. By the end of the melee, 34 people were dead.

The summer of 1967 also saw riots in many American cities. The biggest of these uprisings was again in Detroit. Eighty-two people were arrested in a night raid on illegal gambling dens. At the sight of the arrests, passersby became enraged and stoned the police. The next day crowds of thousands began to smash and loot businesses in the ghetto. Police were driven out of the area. Then the National Guard was called in to restore order, but many of the soldiers lost control and took wild shots at people. This further enraged the residents. Sniping broke out. As the trouble grew worse, federal paratroopers were called out. Large areas of the city were reduced to burned-out hulks. Mob violence was matched by mass arrest, rough treatment, and beatings. Altogether, about 40 ghetto dwellers were killed and more than 7,000 arrested. The people of the ghetto expressed their frustration with being poor, unemployed, and discriminated against by destroying much of the area in which they themselves lived.

Ghetto riots appear to be spontaneous expressions of rage; protests are usually well organized and nonviolent in intent. Nevertheless, protest demonstrations often generate violence because they attract opposition.

In the past decade, protests grew out of two major concerns: civil rights and the Vietnam antiwar movement. Never in U.S. history had a war been more frequently or persistently objected to than the lengthy Vietnam affair. Not since the draft riots of 1863 had so many people cried out against a government policy. The late 1960s and early 1970s saw thousands of people march for and against the war, provoke (and be provoked into) brawls, fight with police or find themselves at the wrong end of short police tempers.

Civil rights conflicts have continued to the present, although in a muted form as compared with the sixties. Women, blacks, Indians, Mexican-Americans, and other groups with grievances have marched, engaged in sit-ins and strikes to try to better their condition or right injustices in American society.

In recent years, the level and intensity of American violence seems to have subsided. Yet there are numerous, often daily examples of child abuse, drunken brawls, murder, suicide, prison conflict, ecological destruction, syndicate activity, and protests of one sort or another. Occasionally, extremist political groups bait and bomb other groups or organizations they hate. Strange and flamboyant kidnappings, such as that of Patricia Hearst in California, occur from time to time. So do clashes between ethnic and racial groups, between police and ghetto dwellers, between one youth gang and another. People worry about crime in the streets and safety in the home.

Many people view the United States as an inherently violent culture, a culture intrigued by conflict and prone to participate in it. Periods of relative calm may be due to chance or minor social or political changes, but violence lies just beneath the surface. Some argue that our society, as it has become more populous and urbanized, has grown deeply impersonal. Our sense of being is destroyed, making us insensitive to the needs of others and unwilling to help or protect one another.

Others disagree with this view. They feel that the nature or type of violence has changed. These people point out that feuds have almost vanished; that political violence is rare; that respect for law has increased; that the mentally ill are treated humanely rather than as devils or criminals; that bloody strikes are a thing of the past. Many Americans feel that some sorts of violence are helpful, especially if the lot of the poor or blacks or some other minority group is improved. Some people maintain that we are less violent as a people than other nationalities have been; that if we are guilty of violence, so is the rest of the human race. Considering only the recent past, the systematic elimination of the opposition during the Stalinist era in Russia; the enormity of the Nazi German extermination of 6 million Jews; the hundreds of thousands murdered for religious reasons during the partition of India in 1947; and the barbarisms committed during the separation of Bangladesh from Pakistan—these are examples of the wholesale slaughter of human beings by other beings that staggers the imagination. Savage destruction of the "enemy" within or without can be found in the history of almost every nation in the world. Are Americans more or less violent than others—or are all people violent by nature? The remaining chapters in this book will give you some further ideas to think about.

What Do You Think?

1. Is the United States an inherently violent country? More so than other countries?

2. Has violence lessened over the centuries? Increased? How can we tell?

3. Have the types and causes of violence changed with different periods of history? Or have early trends continued? Give examples to support your opinion.

4. Are some forms of violence constructive? If so, which types? If not, why not?

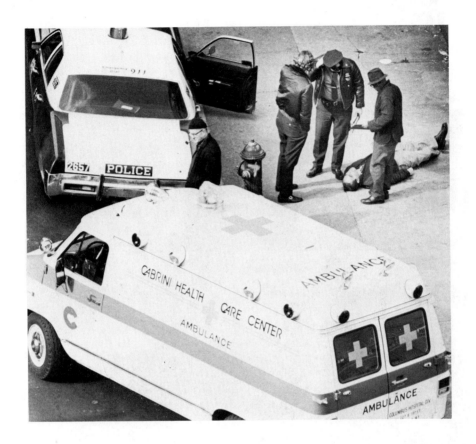

3
WHAT
IS
VIOLENCE?

If a man kills his neighbor during a quarrel, the violence involved is clear to everyone. Most people would add murder, rape, warfare, beating, and torture to this list of aggressive human behaviors. But is this concept of violence broad enough? Even where physical violence develops, it may take many forms, each different from the others. One type might be brutal but organized and legitimate, such as a prize fight or a rough football game—or the violence could be wild and emotional, like a riot. All of these examples are open for people to see and judge.

But perhaps there are more subtle kinds of violence—where people damage each other's souls or minds. Such violence is hard to see, and its impact difficult to determine. What you see as violent depends a great deal on your definition of the term. As you read the articles in this chapter, determine the form of violence being illustrated and how it injures the people involved. What is *your* definition of violence?

1. The Ludlow Massacre*

In April 1914, at Ludlow, Colorado, state militia and miners clashed in a small-scale war. The miners were seeking recognition of their union and freedom from company domination. This song by folk singer Woody Guthrie commemorates the event. What does it tell you about labor violence of the early twentieth century? Does this kind of violence exist today?

It was early springtime when the strike was on,
They drove us miners out of doors,
Out from the houses that the company owned;
We moved into tents up at old Ludlow.

I was worried bad about my children,
Soldiers guarding the railroad bridge;

Every once in a while the bullets would fly,
Kick up gravel under my feet.

We were so afraid you would kill our children,
We dug us a cave that was seven foot deep,
Carried our young ones and a pregnant woman
Down inside the cave to sleep.

That very night you soldiers waited,
Until us miners was asleep;
You snuck around our little tent town,
Soaked our tents with your kerosene.

You struck a match and the blaze it started;
You pulled the triggers of your Gatling guns;
I made a run for the children but the fire wall stopped me,
Thirteen children died from your guns.

I carried my blanket to a wire fence corner,
Watched the fire till the blaze died down;
I helped some people grab their belongings,
While your bullets killed us all around.

I never will forget the look on the face,
Of the men and women that awful day,
When we stood around to preach their funerals
And lay the corpses of the dead away.

We told the Colorado governor to phone the President,
Tell him to call off his National Guard;
But the National Guard belonged to the Governor,
So he didn't try so very hard.

Our women from Trinidad they hauled some potatoes
Up to Walsenburg in a little cart;
They sold their potatoes and brought some guns back
And they put a gun in every hand.

The state soldiers jumped us in the wire fence corner;
They did not know that we had these guns.
And the red-neck miners mowed down these troopers,
You should have seen those poor boys run.

We took some cement and walled the cave up
Where you killed these thirteen children inside;
I said "God bless the mine workers' union,"
And then I hung my head and cried.

1. How does this example compare to other strikes you have read or heard about?
2. Why would someone write a song about a strike?

2. Child Abuse*

When parents are immature, disturbed, even psychotic, children may become the most convenient object for the venting of frustration. What can be done to prevent the "battered child syndrome"?

Danny and Patrick Noble were 5 and 7, respectively, when they came to public attention. A neighbor reported to a social welfare agency that Mr. Noble, in her opinion, beat his children with excessive brutality, far beyond what was needed to keep such passive little boys in line. She hated to make such a report because the Nobles seemed to be such wholesome, decent people, but she felt that someone ought to talk to them about the way they were handling their children.

Mr. Noble, appearing at the agency without his wife, looked like a fine person. He was well-dressed, well-educated, self-assured, and gainfully employed in an executive position. There was nothing he wouldn't do for his family, he said. He admitted that he disciplined his children but explained that he was obliged to teach them obedience because his wife indulged them too much.

Patient questioning elicited the fact that the last time he had disciplined Danny, the boy had ended up locked in the basement, lying at the bottom of the stairs with a broken leg.

Eight-year-old Mike Roberts was reported by the admitting physician at the county hospital to have been treated for lacerations, bruises, burn-like welts, and a broken arm. Investigation revealed that his injuries had been inflicted by his mother with a broomstick and the cord of a electric appliance, and that the attack was only the latest in a series. Mrs. Roberts could not understand why people were making such a fuss about it, Mike was HER son and her business.

Children of Fear

Enough? More than enough? But this is only a skimpy sampling, a skimming from the surface of a truly terrible reality which seems to be coldly trapped on the printed page instead of screaming for attention as it should.

---

*Vincent J. Fontana, *Somewhere a Child Is Crying,* Long Island Press, 1973. Copyright © 1973 by Vincent J. Fontana.

These are children chained in torture chambers from which they cannot free themselves.

Is it possible to be clinically objective, not to think of the dreadful loneliness, the isolation, the helplessness, the terror, or the pain? Imagine the awful fear and anguish of a child whose parents are his enemies, of a child who has been burnt and beaten and knows that he will be burnt and beaten again. Is it worse to long for a loving touch and never receive it or cringe before a raised fist?

It has got to make more sense, if there is any humanity in us, to find ways to improve the quality of human life. . . .

Stopping the Syndrome

Unfortunately, it is not difficult to find an endless string of cases illustrative of physical abuse and neglect. What is difficult to pinpoint and describe is the more subtle maltreatment at which some parents are adept.

There are parental attitudes as damaging as a push down stairs or a command to get "the hell out of the house" because mother's got company. There are the broken homes, the parade of "fathers," the constant moves and changes of school, the cold shouldering, the lack of guidance, the absence of standards, the excess of discipline or total lack of it, the verbal contempt, the hurtful language, the total inability to recognize a child as a human being with rights or to accept a child as a child.

These are the insidious wounds with the invisible scars, scars that become visible as the child grows into adulthood. These victims, as children, may never see the inside of a hospital emergency room or a youth shelter; but these victims, as adults, have every good chance of winding up on the psychiatrist's couch, or in family court on neglect or abuse charges, or behind bars for a violent crime.

Many maltreated children are children who were very much wanted before birth. Perhaps they were wanted for the wrong reasons: to give the mother something of her own to love and give her love in return; to cement a couple on the verge of separation; to present a picture of a conventional family unit because for one reason or other that is the expected or respectable thing to do.

Immature people, emotionally starved people, abused people, neurotic people, deprived people, more often than not, sincerely want their children. It is only after the children arrive that the doubts set in and the problems surface.

A good many parents, in the act of abusing their children, are in the grip of an uncontrollable anger and a love-hate emotion that has nothing to do with wanting the children and not wanting to love them. . . .

What Do You Think? _____

1. **How far do parents' rights extend in the matter of control and discipline of children?**

2. Is there a difference between punishment and mistreatment? Explain.

3. What kinds of parental actions would you consider violent? Nonviolent? Why?

---

3. Violence to the Environment*

People often treat their environment as a giant garbage dump. Can destruction of the environment be classed as violence?

Gooey Horror Oozing Toward N.Y.

Just over the horizon from this rocky point, covering the seabed for 20 square miles, one of the world's great environmental horrors may be preparing to turn on the people who created it.

It is called the "Dead Sea" and it is there, 12 miles offshore that New York and surrounding cities have dumped their sewage sludge—about 5 million cubic yards a year—for four decades.

For miles in any direction from the site the sea floor is covered with stuff that one scientist described as resembling black mayonnaise. It is toxic, smells like rotten eggs and contains huge counts of fecal coliform bacteria as well as the viruses of hepatitis, encephalitis, and other diseases.

Because the dumping ground was so far out to sea, the city believed it would never hear from its sludge again, but the city was wrong. The mass of goo slowly grew and sometime around 1970 it began to move, oozing back to haunt New York and the beaches of Long Island.

Several studies are under way. Scientists are sinking sampling devices to the seabed to analyze the contents for organic matter and concentrations of heavy metals, two of the principal ingredients of sludge.

These studies have placed the leading edge of the sludge at about 3½ miles from the Long Island beaches, although one recent expedition found a small bed only half a mile away. Three years ago the sludge was approximately eight miles from the beaches.

"We're not sure why it's moving and we're not sure when it started," said William H. Harris, a marine geologist from Brooklyn College, who is directing a study for New York City Institute of Oceanography. "But in my own mind I feel there's a good chance the stuff will hit the beaches in three years."

Although Harris stresses that further study will be required, he said the sludge movement may have begun when the dump site simply filled up, causing further dumping to spread outward with ocean currents.

The center of the "Dead Sea" area has long been a source of fascination and horror to environmentalists. During Earth Week in 1971 it was voted as one of the top ten ecological disasters in the world.

*San Francisco Chronicle, 1974.

In its center, nothing lives. The goo, which is allowed to settle in primary treatment plants before dumping, contains industrial waste, pesticides, detergents and other solvents as well as human and animal fecal matter.

Rotting debris bobs the surface and the ocean at times takes on varying hues of dark green, light brown or black.

A federal report released in 1972 said many lobsters and crabs collected near the site were found to be diseased. Fish were found with their fins rotting off.

The site collects the concentrated sewage of more than 13 million persons in the New York Metropolitan area.

What Do You Think?

1. Could the "Dead Sea" of this article have been prevented? If so, how?
2. Is any abuse of the environment, however large or small, an act of violence?

4. Economic Violence*

Sometimes organizations, unions, and other groups go out on strike. Strikes frequently become violent. Here is an example.

Jobs and Deliveries of Food Threatened As Independent Drivers Press Stoppage

Scattered gunfire and reduced truck traffic were reported yesterday as independent truckers forged ahead with a work stoppage that threatened jobs and deliveries of fresh food.

Truckers attempting to go about their business despite the strikers' demands reported being shot at in Virginia, Missouri, Tennessee, Texas and Ohio. A woman trucker in Ohio said that she had been pulled from her vehicle and beaten until two nonstriking drivers arrived armed with a shotgun.

Some 200 Pennsylvania National Guardsmen stood watch over highway overpasses in an effort to protect trucks from attack. One driver was killed in Pennsylvania Thursday when a boulder was dropped on his cab from an overpass.

The Armour Food Company announced that it was closing or curtailing operations at seven meat-packing plants. The General Electric Company shut down one plant and two Philadelphia slaughterhouses closed.

*From "Truckers Report Shots in Five States," © 1974 by The New York Times Company. Reprinted by permission.

One of the Southeast's biggest truck stops, Perlis Truck Stop in Cordele, Ga., was nearly abandoned. A cashier, Jimmy House, said that only 1,100 gallons of fuel were pumped during the night, against an average of 10,000 gallons.

Most of the predawn violence yesterday involved shots fired at trucks, vandalism to vehicles at truck stops and threats to drivers defying the walkout call.

At issue are demands by independent drivers for guaranteed lower fuel prices and increased freight rates. Diesel fuel prices have risen from 20 cents a gallon to nearly 50 cents in some areas.

What Do You Think?

1. What produced this truckers' strike?
2. Why are some strikes *not* violent?

---

5. Violence in Sports

Most people think sports are mainly for fun. But look at the following pictures.

What Do You Think?

1. Must sport be violent? Always?
2. Is violence as part of a game any less or more serious than other forms of conflict? Why or why not?

6. Vandalism*

Vandalism usually involves the destruction of property. However, in the story that follows it takes on special meaning because of the neighborhood in which it took place. Why have these people been vandalized?

"All we can do is wonder what will happen next!"

Norman English made the comment yesterday after viewing the vandalism in the front yard of his home at 109-42 215th St., Queens Village.

During the past two years, English has had the tires of his car slashed twice and yesterday there was a sign on his front gate as well as green paint splattered over his blue and white car and over the front yard.

The sign read: "We Hate Negro's—N.R.T.G.B.O.O.Q.V."

Police say the initials at the bottom of the hand-written sign on the back

*Excerpted from Hal Shapiro, "Vandalism Mystery Probed by Police," *Long Island Press,* August 5, 1971.

of a piece of cardboard measuring 1 X 1½ feet could stand for New Radicals To Get Blacks Out of Queens Village.

* * * * *

English and his wife, Ena, are natives of Jamaica in the British West Indies.

They speak with a marked British accent.

"We've been living here for four years," Mrs. English said, "and the neighbors have been very nice. I work as a registered nurse and also attend Hunter College, so I don't spend much time at home.

"Our two sons—Richard Bruce, 13, and 7-year-old Robert Brent—attend SS Joachim and Anne Parochial School along with most of the children on the block. Our street is well integrated with both blacks and whites, although we are the only West Indians here.

"We have finished the basement of our home and my sons play with the other children, both black and white. I don't understand what is going on."

English, an accountant, said he and his family are trying to live decently but that people are "trying to turn us into some kind of animals."

* * * * *

His wife said the first incident of tire slashing occurred about a year and a half ago, and the second time was about two months ago. Neither incident was reported to police.

"Other cars in the neighborhood also had tires slashed so we didn't feel the first time that it was aimed against us," Mrs. English said. "The second time we found the knife that was used, but we figured it best that we just get the tires replaced.

"When our tenant told us about the latest incident, however, at 7:10 A.M. yesterday we called the police."

The tenant, Rawle Ford, is also a West Indian.

The sign was hanging on the gate in front of the house facing the entrance.

"From what I see now," English said, "it looks as though whatever is going on is directed against me. And it looks like they mean business."

The English's neighbors are also mystified about the vandalism.

* * * * *

Anthony Delaney, who lives a couple of doors away, thought it might be the work of a group of real estate dealers who have been trying to get the residents on the quiet tree-lined street to move out.

"During the past couple of weeks these guys have been coming into this block and ringing doorbells," Delaney said.

"They give us all the same line that they've heard we want to sell our homes. Nothing could be further from the truth."

Delaney said there aren't any problems on the block.

"There is no animosity here," he declared. "We have always had good relations. Everyone is proud of their neighborhood."

1. Can destruction of property be considered violence? Why or why not?

2. Might other types of violence come about as a result of vandalism like that described in this article? Explain.

3. Can this sort of thing be stopped? If so, how?

4. Some vandalism is not directed against specific people or places but seems to be more or less random. What might cause this kind of destructive behavior?

---

7. Assassination*

Political leaders are sometimes hated by groups or individuals who disagree strongly with their views. Most people are content to express their disagreement verbally—but some are not.

It was George Wallace's kind of afternoon—the sun suddenly ablaze, the crowd numerous and happy, the biggest day of his upstart primary campaign and maybe his whole political life only a tomorrow away. "Send 'em a message," he hollered across the asphalt plains of the Laurel Shopping Center; "give 'em a case of Saint Vitus dance." And then he came down from behind his armor-plated lectern, shucked his coat, whispered with his security people and moved out to work the rope and meet the folk and keep his date with the blond man.

The blond man had been waiting for weeks—had tagged along in the shadows of the Wallace cavalcade in a dusty blue Rambler with a library of road maps and a snub-nosed .38 and a toneless grin that could turn spring into winter. He was standing in the second row on the lot in Laurel when Wallace came by grabbing at hands and receiving the love of the faithful. Somebody was telling the governor he had their vote, and the governor was smiling back and saying, "Thank you, and tell—." He never finished. The .38 poked out between two spectators in the front row, so close that the heat of it stung them when the shooting started. There was a pop-pop-pop-pop-pop and people were clawing and spinning and falling. George Wallace landed flat out on the asphalt, his eyes blank, his legs lifeless. The blond man went under, a flying wedge of cops taking him away from the crowd, and when they hauled him off purpling under a strangle hold, he was still grinning that flat wintry grin.

They found out later that the blond man was Arthur Herman Bremer, a 5-foot 6-inch psychic shut-in of 21 out of ethnic Milwaukee with no trade, no girl, no known radical connections, no discernible ideology at all—nothing

*"Appointment in Laurel," Copyright © Newsweek, Inc., 1972, reprinted by permission.

but a clear and growing vocation for trouble. In the days following the shooting, people began remembering having seen him here and there along the trail, poking around at Wallace functions, grinning eerily out of the front ranks at Wallace rallies in his red, white and blue shirt and his rumpled suit with a Wallace lapel button. Artie Bremer, as it developed, was memorable only in sad retrospect—only after he had crippled George Wallace, transformed the politics of 1972 and thrown the dark shadow of violence once again across the American political process.

His motive was locked away in the jangled circuits of his mind; there was only the tantalizing suggestion that his date with Wallace was set the day he and his 16-year old girl friend broke up last January. The governor announced formally for President in the middle of their crise. Bremer, taking the breakup hard, shaved his head, bought the snubnosed, five-shot "Undercover 2" revolver at a shop called Casanova Guns, Inc., and began the long turn inward that ended on the parking lot at Laurel. He picked up some Republican campaign buttons, and once, in April, he checked into the Waldorf-Astoria Hotel, in New York, on a night when Hubert Humphrey was supposed to be staying there. (Humphrey did not.) But his interest seemed to fasten on the Alabama governor and his rebel Democratic campaign. Bremer plastered a Wallace sticker across his apartment house door. He looked in on Wallace gatherings in Milwaukee during the Wisconsin primary campaign, or so the governor's staff remembered. He wrote notes to himself—one a vaguely hostile scrawl about Wallace, another wishing: "Cheer up Oswald."

What Do You Think?———————————————————————————

Is assassination ever justified? Explain.

---

8. Violence Against the Spirit*

Next, a semifictional description of daily life among poor people living in the slums on the West side of New York. Are the people in this account being subjected to violence?

January 22. There are enough pages in this diary for me to write something every day. But there isn't something to write every day. We have one room in this building on West 104th Street. On 118th Street we had three rooms. There was no hot water or heat in the building on 118th Street for five weeks. The landlord said the boiler broke and he didn't have money to get

*Reprinted by permission of Coward, McCann & Geoghegan, Inc., from *The Diary of A.N.* by Julius Horwitz, 1970. Copyright © 1970 by Julius Horwitz.

it fixed. Momma boiled hot water on the gas stove and we kept the burners going day and night. Momma stuffed up all the windows to keep the heat in but I remembered from school that gas could kill you if you didn't have air and so I always kept one window just a little bit open. Some of the people in the building wanted to kill the landlord. But others said it would do no good. Momma kept me out of school so that she could go looking for an apartment for us. She went out every morning at nine o'clock and would come home when it was dark. She would be mad and yelling, saying there had to be a place in the city for us to live. She said there was no living on West 118th Street. Just cold, fights, screaming people. What Momma says is right but the way we live seems to be all wrong.

January 24. Now I wonder if we should have moved. The cold would have gone away on 118th Street and there we had three rooms. Here on 104th Street we have one room and not even a big room. The room is filled by the two beds where we all sleep, a small refrigerator, a small gas stove. The toilet and bathroom is in the hallway and all the families on this side of the hallway use it. This means 9 families. I counted how many people there are in the 9 families and the number is 47 and with our family it is 52. For two days the toilet was broken. Momma told us to go at school. The bathtub doesn't work in the hall toilet. Momma bought a round plastic tub that we put on the floor and we take a bath with a sponge and hot water.

Momma says we won't stay in this building long. She said it was the only place she could find where they would take five people. Even Edgar is counted as a person. I wish the rats would know this. For the last two nights we have taken turns staying awake to see that none of the rats get to bite Edgar. Momma said we should look for the holes where the rats come from and then we can nail wood or flattened-out tin cans over the holes in the wall. I saw one rat come out from under the wall and he came for Edgar's crib and I threw the rolled up newspaper Momma gave me at the rat. We had rats on West 118th Street. Harriet woke up one night on 118th screaming that something was chewing on the toes of her feet and Momma jumped out of bed and began beating at the rat with a rolled up Life magazine.

This building seems to have more rats than all of the buildings that we have lived in that I remember. Maybe it's because of all the people and all the babies. The garbage piles up in all the hallways. Sometimes it's not taken down all day. Rats eat garbage. In school they say the way to get rid of rats is to starve them.

What Do You Think?

1. By allowing conditions such as the ones described in this article to exist, is society doing violence to poor people? Explain.
2. Why do conditions such as these exist?

9. "Warehouses of Degradation"*

Recent events, such as prison riots in several cities, have caused many to doubt the effectiveness of prisons as corrective institutions. The article that follows, written by a former U.S. Attorney General, presents a view that is becoming more and more frequently expressed. What kinds of violence does the author describe?

Dostoievsky called the book he wrote about his years in prison in Siberia "The House of the Dead" with reason. If he died and awoke in hell, he wrote, he would expect it to be no worse than the prisoners' bathhouse—a filthy, stinking hole filled with dense steam and hundreds of naked bodies. On his last night in prison, walking along the fence that had confined him for four years, he concluded that, on the whole, the men there were no better and no worse than people generally. Among them were exceptionally strong and gifted people; the waste of their lives was an intolerable cruelty. From this experience he defined man as "a creature that can become accustomed to anything."

It sometimes seems that prisons try to disprove Dostoievsky's definition by brutalizing beyond the ability of man to bear. Here in the United States,

*Playboy, excerpted from Ramsey Clark, "When Punishment Is a Crime," 1970. Copyright © 1970 by Ramsey Clark. Reprinted by permission of Simon and Schuster.

jails and prisons are usually little more than warehouses of human degradation. More often than not, they manufacture crime rather than discourage it. Ninety-five percent of all the expenditures in the entire field of correction in this country goes for custody—iron bars, stone walls, guards. Five percent goes for health services, education, developing employment skills—for hope.

A look at prison custody at its worst was afforded by the 1968 investigation of the Cummins and Tucker prison farms in Arkansas. Discipline was maintained largely by prisoners themselves—trusties with shotguns—working under a handful of paid employees. It was alleged that inmates were beaten, shot, murdered. Broken bodies were uncovered in shallow graves. Food unfit to eat was regularly served. Forced homosexuality was openly tolerated. Wardens allegedly extorted money and sexual favors from inmates' families. Prisoners were reportedly tortured. . . .

It would be difficult to devise a better method of draining the last drop of compassion from a human being than confinement in most prisons as they exist today. In many of them, there are large dormitory rooms with 100 beds or more, where guards do not venture at night. Violence cannot be controlled in such an area. Beatings, deaths and suicides are frequent. Rape and homosexual cultures involve most of the inmates by choice or force. In a climate of fear and violence, many wardens work only to avoid the general disorder that can wreck their prisons. They are so relieved to see the most dangerous and violent prisoners go that they sometimes release such men in disregard of public safety.

If prisons offer any work at all, it is generally meaningless or obsolete. Most prisoners in youth centers are school dropouts, yet only a few have a chance to continue their schooling while imprisoned. Studies have shown that most prisoners suffer from some mental disturbance at the time they commit their crime, but treatment for mental illness in prisons is virtually nonexistent. More men have mental-health problems on leaving prison than on entering. Psychotics are frequently left for the inmates to control, and sometimes it is the psychotics who control.

Simple physical illnesses generally are poorly treated in prison, if they are treated at all. For example, because they have poor backgrounds, most prisoners have never had any dentalwork and badly need it, but few get adequate attention in prison. Personalities are shaped by such factors as the loss of teeth. While that loss is but one of many disadvantages and only a part of a dehumanizing existence, it adds its measure of brutalization. Human dignity is lost. Finally, drug usage is common in prison and many men become addicted there.

It is one of the greater ironies of our time that, concerned as we are about crime, we so neglect the one area within the whole system of criminal justice that offers the best opportunity to cut the crime rate. The most important crime statistic is that 80 percent of all felonies are committed by repeaters. That is, four fifths of our major crimes are committed by people who are already known to the criminal-justice system. We have demonstrated that we can cut recidivism—the repetition of crime by individuals—in half where we make the effort to do so. In fact, under the best of conditions, we could cut

recidivism far more than that. If we are truly concerned about crime—if we really care about our own character—how can we fail to make the massive effort called for?

Correction, in its entire range of services—from pretrial detention in jail through the parole system—has been debilitated by neglect. In general, our local jails are manned by untrained people. Prisons are usually located in remote areas, where it is difficult to attract personnel with professional skills or to retain those that do have them. In both jails and prisons, salaries are so low, working conditions so unpleasant and opportunity for advancement so limited that few people want to work in them. Many of those who could accomplish the most in correction are frightened away by the present deplorable conditions. Some of those attracted to guard duty today have an unhealthy urge for authority over people; many more prison guards are gradually made brutal by the environment of the prison itself, something that might happen to anyone.

What Do You Think?

1. The author states that prisons more often than not "manufacture crime rather than discourage it." What does he mean? Would this hold true for violence as well? Why or why not?

2. How would you explain the idea that "concerned as we are about crime, we so neglect the one area within the whole system of criminal justice that offers the best opportunity to cut the crime rate"? Do you agree or disagree? Why?

10. The Electricity Was Turned Off

An electric company turns off a couple's power during mid-winter for nonpayment of bills. They die from the cold soon after. Has anyone committed an act of violence in this example?

Elderly Couple Died After Heat Shut Off*

A medical examiner said yesterday an elderly couple found dead in their unheated home Christmas Eve died of "circulatory collapse secondary to exposure to the cold."

The bodies of Frank Baker, 93, and his wife, Catherine, 92, were discovered four days after Niagara Mohawk Power Corp. said it turned off electricity to the couple's home because they refused to settle $250 in back bills.

"There's no question that this is the cause of death," said Dr. Robert J. Sullivan, Schenectady County medical examiner.

"Everything we can gather points to this. There was no food in their stomachs or liquids or drugs. We also analyzed the urine for substances that were foreign to the human. There was no carbon monoxide."

A spokesman for Niagara Mohawk said the utility had no comment.

"We don't see how we can properly comment on a medical finding," the spokesman said. "All that we can really say is that we intend to cooperate fully with any governmental agencies which are investigating."

There was no immediate statement from Schenectady Dist. Atty. Albert Watrous, who said earlier he had delayed a decision regarding possible court action against Niagara Mohawk because he had no facts that would indicate a negligent homicide charge should be placed.

*   *   *   *   *

Sullivan said the Bakers had died within a short time of each other, and had been dead two to four days before they were found.

"The man was lying somewhat across his wife," the medical examiner said. "You might guess he was trying to protect her."

Deaths by Freezing Stir Calls for Laws**

Calls for the kind of legislation that might have prevented the death by freezing of an elderly couple were made by city officials and civic groups today as investigations—some aimed at a possible indictment of the Niagara Mohawk Power Corporation—were started.

The company, which turned off the couple's electricity last Thursday for

*"Elderly Couple Died After Heat Shut Off," *Long Island Press,* 1974.
**Copyright © 1973 by The New York Times Company. Reprinted by permission.

nonpayment of a $250 electric bill, expressed regret but denied responsibility for the deaths.

"We're running a business," a spokesman for the company said. "The welfare people should have been taking care of them."

The bodies of the couple—93-year old Frank Baker and his 92-year old wife, Catherine—were found on Christmas Eve huddled together on the floor of the ramshackle frame home in the dilapidated Hamilton Hill section here. For almost a week, nighttime temperatures had been near zero.

Dr. John L. Shields, the deputy medical examiner, said today that autopsies had found nothing inconsistent with his original tentative pronouncement of death due to exposure to cold. But he said the final determination would have to await tests to be made next week.

Albert Watrous Jr., the Schenectady County District Attorney, said that he did not want to accuse Niagara Mohawk without a complete investigation but that a grand jury investigation was possible within the week.

"The State Public Utilities Commission has demanded an explanation of them," he said, "and I'm sure we'll all want to wait for all the facts before anybody does anything."

What the commission, the District Attorney, the Police Dept. and a number of civic groups wanted to know is whether criminal negligence and violations of state utility regulations were involved in turning off power to the couple's home.

The utility said today that it had acted properly and that it welcomed the investigations.

"There are cases," according to Ralph Van Woert, manager of the company's capital area, "where circumstances indicate potential threats to health and safety. In this case, we made every effort to avoid discontinuance of service. We did not deem it necessary to deviate from our normal collection procedures as a result of our repeated experiences with Mr. Baker over the past several years."

He said a company representative spoke with Mr. Baker on Dec. 13, a week before the power was turned off but found him unresponsive, as he had been during the numerous times in the past when bills were overdue and power was cut off.

The Bakers' electricity was turned off for a month six months ago for nonpayment of a $250 bill, but part of the sum was paid by a church group, and service was restored.

"They were very, very fiercely independent people," recalled Dorr A. Spencer, president of the St. Vincent de Paul Society of the St. Columba's Roman Catholic Church, around the corner from the Baker home, which raised the money.

"We could have forced our way in there this time if we had known about it," he said, "but perhaps they died in dignity."

The police said they found money in the couple's home today; according to The Associated Press Detective Edward O'Connor refused to disclose the amount but said it was less than $1,000. Some of the money, found under mattresses and wrapped in toilet paper, was in $10 and $20 bills, it was said.

What Do You Think? _____

1. What is violence—the Power Company turning off your electricity? In winter? If you are old? Sick? Broke?
2. Is not caring about your fellows violence?
3. Who was at fault here—the couple for not paying their bills or the company for cutting the power?

ACTIVITIES FOR INVOLVEMENT

1. Make a list of reasons opposing or supporting each of the following statements:
   a. All violence is wrong.
   b. Might makes right; therefore all violence, force, and coercion is to the good.
   c. Violence should be used only when absolutely necessary as a last resort.
   d. Violence and force are needed to control people and should be used frequently to promote law and order.
   e. Violence is often wrong, and often right—wrong if its effect is destructive, right if its effect is constructive.

   Hold a class discussion as to what groups of people would be most likely to support each statement. Why would this be so?

2. Explain which of the following situations, if any, merit the use of violence.
   a. A senator votes for a very unpopular law. Someone tries to assassinate him.
   b. A pickpocket takes a man's wallet on a bus. Several other men see this, grab the pickpocket, and beat him severely until he returns the wallet.
   c. Several slum tenants have their rent raised. They refuse to pay and are evicted by the landlord. At night, they return and blow up the building. The structure is demolished, but no people are in it at the time of the blast.
   d. Members of two ethnic groups are engaged in a brawl in a public park. Police arrive and tear gas the brawlers. Several continue fighting and are clubbed until they stop.
   e. A member of a crime syndicate is tortured by police until he tells many of his group's secrets. This information leads to the arrest of several drug pushers, professional murderers, and racketeers.
   f. A child burns a neighbor's dog, crippling it. The parents, after finding out about this, spank the child until he is black and blue.

3. Hold a hypothetical round-table discussion in which various students roleplay authors you have read in this chapter and discuss their reactions to each of the situations in Activity 2 above.

4. Read the views of Martin Luther King in *Where Do We Go From Here* and Mahatma Gandhi in *Non-Violent Resistance* on violence and nonviolent protest. Report on their view to the class. Then read the views of Bobby Seale, Malcolm X, and Herbert Marcuse on violence and revolution. Compare these views with those of the previous set of authors, and again report to the class. Which author(s) would you support? Why? Be prepared to defend your position.

5. Invite a pacifist to speak to the class about the philosophy of total nonviolence. Take notes on the point of view given, and later hold a debate on the proposition that, "All use of force and violence for any end, even self-defense, is morally wrong."

6. Do some research and gather information about some of the factors that you think cause violence in America (e.g., poverty, discrimination, racism, criminality, mental illness, political powerlessness). Make a list of possible violent and nonviolent ways of dealing with each factor and then rank them in order from least to most effective. Explain why you think some means are better than others. Type up your list of factors and your suggestions for dealing with each in the form of a questionnaire. For instance, one factor might look something like this:

Factor	Possible Solutions	Effective Scale
Poverty	1. Organize and vote for the candidate who will work for better housing, jobs, and rights for the poor	1 2 3 4 5
	2. Loot and steal from the wealthy, from government, and from businesses	1 2 3 4 5
	3. March and demonstrate regularly against job discrimination, low welfare payments, and segregated housing	1 2 3 4 5
	4. Kidnap wealthy people and hold them for ransom	1 2 3 4 5
	5. Join a pressure group to lobby for actions and laws you desire	1 2 3 4 5
	6. Cop out from society and do what you want to do, not caring about others	1 2 3 4 5

Ask those taking the poll (starting with your classmates) to circle the number best representing their beliefs about the effectiveness of certain actions over others. Let 1 stand for low effectiveness and 5 for high effectiveness, with other ratings in between. Which ideas seem most supported? Least? How would you explain these findings?

7. *Joe:* Human life is sacred. The preservation of life is more important than anything else.

Mary: I believe in living, but I think that life should be happy; life alone is not enough.

John: You both have good ideas, but I really don't think people always have to be happy or should preserve life at any cost. What is most important is justice; people should treat each other fairly.

Each of these students has expressed an idea that is also a value: It tells what each person thinks is most worthwhile. Whose value would you agree with? Why? Whose would you disagree with? Why?

Develop an argument for the value you most closely agree with and find examples to support your judgment. After you have chosen a position and constructed an argument, discuss the following questions:

    a.   Under which value would violence as a method for change be considered most wrong? Why?

    b.   Which value seems most likely to condone or allow for violence? Why?

    c.   What are the implications of each goal of man for violence: life, happiness, or justice? (Consider both offensive and defensive violence.)

8.   Complete the above discussion by drawing up a list of standards or guidelines for studying violence to help you decide when, if ever, it is justified and when it is not. Using your standards, how would you decide the following cases:

    a.   Mercy killing

    b.   Hurting or killing an enemy in war

    c.   Fighting with a burglar

    d.   Threatening another person

    e.   "Doing what you are told"

    f.   Making fun of others

    g.   Protesting poverty

    h.   Looting

4
WHAT ARE THE CAUSES OF VIOLENCE?

There are many theories about the causes of violence. One popular line of thought holds that humanity is inherently aggressive. When people want their way, either as a group or as individuals, they use many means, including violence, to obtain it. It is an integral part of human personality and can no more be controlled than can the motion of the planets.

Another line of thought argues that people become violent for specific reasons, and that nearly all of these reasons have a social and personal motivation. They point out that people in different times, in different places, and in different social positions do not exhibit the same rates, amounts, or degrees of violence. Different social conditions produce more or less conflict and different forms of violence.

Within this latter view of violence, there are many opinions as to which conditions in society are most likely to prevent violence and which conditions are most likely to contribute to it.

As you read the following articles, note the various causes that the authors present. Which causes seem most significant to you?

1. The Dictates of Conscience*

In this selection, Henry David Thoreau, of Walden *fame, defends the spirit and the actions of John Brown, the abolitionist who raided Harper's Ferry in 1859. Brown and his men sized the federal arsenal to arm the slaves for rebellion, but the plot failed. He was later captured and hanged by the U.S. government for his actions. Many people felt that Brown was insane; Thoreau, however, disagreed. Thoreau used the example of John Brown to raise questions about law and conscience. What are these questions? What is their implication for violence?*

Any man knows when he is justified, and all the wits in the world cannot enlighten him on that point. The murderer always knows that he is justly punished; but when a government takes the life of a man without the consent of his conscience, it is an audacious[1] government, and is taking a step towards its own dissolution. Is it not possible that an individual may be right and a government wrong? Are laws to be enforced simply because they were made? or declared by any number of men to be good, if they are *not* good? Is there any necessity for a man's being a tool to perform a deed of which his better nature disapproves? Is it the intention of lawmakers that *good* men shall be hung ever? Are judges to interpret the law according to the letter, and not the

---

*Excerpted from Henry David Thoreau, "A Plea for Captain John Brown," in *Echoes of Harper's Ferry* by James Redpath. New York: Arno Press, 1969.
36   [1]Daring.

spirit? What right have *you* to enter into a compact with yourself that you *will* do thus or so, against the light within you? Is it for *you* to *make up* your mind—to form any resolution whatever—and not accept the convictions that are forced upon you, and which ever pass your understanding. I do not believe in lawyers, in that mode of attacking or defending a man, because you descend to meet the judge on his own ground, and, in cases of the highest importance, it is of no consequence whether a man breaks a human law or not. Let lawyers decide trivial cases. Business men may arrange that among themselves. If they were the interpreters of the everlasting laws which rightfully bind man, that would be another thing. A counterfeiting law-factory, standing half in a slave land and half in a free! What kinds of laws for free men can you expect from that?

What Do You Think? _____

1. Would you agree or disagree with the idea that breaking a law is sometimes justifiable? If so, when? If not, why not?
2. What does this article suggest as a cause of violence?

---

2. Brain Damage*

Some scientists believe that damage to the brain can produce violent urges and actions. How conclusive does their evidence seem to be?

He was a policeman in Boston, well-liked in his community and known as a good husband and father.

One night at home he handed his wife his gun and told her to lock it up. He felt that his self-control was washing away in a surge of unreasoning rage that he could not explain and might not be able to control. He was afraid that he might shoot someone.

Then he went to his bedroom, handcuffed himself to the bed and stayed there until the rage had burned itself out. The experience was terrifying. It was followed, at intervals, by others just as bad. Then, one day, the same feeling began to sweep over again while he was riding in a police car with two other officers.

*Excerpted from Harold M. Schneck, Jr., "Depths of Brain Probed for Sources of Violence," *The New York Times,* December 27, 1970. Copyright © 1970 by The New York Times Company. Reprinted by permission.

He told them what was happening and begged them to lock him in the back and take him home. They took him to a hospital instead.

200 Studied by Group

Now anticonvulsive drugs keep his attacks largely under control, and he knows why they occur. He had been knocked unconscious in a motorcycle accident six months earlier, and his brain had been injured. The attacks of violent rage were the results of brain damage. It had not occurred to him that his rages were a health problem.

The Boston policeman is one of more than 200 episodically violent men and women who have been treated and studied by a group of medical scientists at Massachusetts General Hospital. Like many other research teams in today's angry world, this group is trying to understand the nature and causes of human violence. . . .

The Boston group is trying to trace the origin and nature of violence to the place where it all begins—the depths of the human brain.

In a few patients who had temporal lobe epilepsy, violent outbreaks have been eliminated, perhaps permanently, by delicate brain surgery. In these operations, small clusters of cells are destroyed by heat from strong electrical stimulation delivered through implanted electrodes. More often, anti-convulsive drugs have been prescribed.

The doctors have turned human attack behavior on and off with an electric switch. They made a motion picture of one patient who erupted into arm-flailing violence when weak, nondestructive electric current was deliberately sent through an electrode planted deep in her brain. The attack stopped just as abruptly when a nearby spot was stimulated.

The behavior was not entirely automatic but was modulated by circumstances of the moment. Dr. Frank R. Ervin, director of the hospital's Stanley Cobb Laboratories of Psychiatric Research, said that the young woman maintained her self-control when her doctors were present but reacted violently when she was alone in the hospital ward. The stimulation was delivered by radio telemetry.

On 12 occasions before she was hospitalized, the young woman had violently assaulted other persons, once almost killing another woman who had accidentally brushed against her arm in a restaurant powder room.

The doctors think that natural, although abnormal, discharges in a damaged brain produced the same effects as the deliberate electrical stimulations. The latter were administered to pinpoint the areas of damage in the patient's temporal lobe in the lower, forward area of the brain. . . .

Dr. Vernon H. Mark, director of neurosurgical services at Boston City Hospital, and Dr. Ervin . . . cite estimates that there are six million Americans who suffer from mental retardation; two million with convulsive disorders, half a million with cerebral palsy, and a substantial, although poorly defined, number of children who are thought to suffer from serious behavior disorders because of impaired brain function.

1. Does the research reported here imply that _all_ aggressive behavior is brought about by biological causes? Most? Only some? What other causes might play a role in man's violent actions?

2. What are your reactions to the general idea of modifying aggressive behavior by controlling the brain? Explain your reasoning. Would your answer be different if the persons involved were dangerous criminals? Explain.

3. Will attacking slums and poverty solve the problem of violence? Why or why not?

---

3. Prejudice*

Riots in large cities are not necessarily something new—as evidenced by the "zoot-suit" riot of 1943 in Los Angeles. Zoot-suits were worn primarily by young people of minority groups and consisted of a loud jacket with wide lapels and very high-waisted trousers. Watches on long gold chains usually completed the outfit. As the incident described below illustrates, wearing such an outfit became dangerous—a crime punishable by mob violence. What does this incident suggest about the causes of violence?

On Monday evening, June seventh, thousands of Angelenos, in response to twelve hours' advance notice in the press, turned out for a mass lynching. Marching through the streets of downtown Los Angeles, a mob of several thousand soldiers, sailors, and civilians, proceeded to beat up every zoot-suiter they could find. Pushing its way into the important motion picture theaters, the mob ordered the management to turn on the house lights and then ranged up and down the aisles dragging Mexicans out of their seats. Street cars were halted while Mexicans, and some Filipinos and Negroes, were jerked out of their seats, pushed into the streets, and beaten with sadistic frenzy. If the victims wore zoot-suits, they were stripped of their clothing and left naked or half-naked on the streets, bleeding and bruised. Proceeding down Main Street from First to Twelfth, the mob stopped on the edge of the Negro district. Learning that the Negroes planned a warm reception for them, the mobsters turned back and marched through the Mexican east side spreading panic and terror. . . .

Throughout the night the Mexican communities were in the wildest possible turmoil. Scores of Mexican mothers were trying to locate their youngsters

*Excerpted from Carey McWilliams, _North From Mexico._ Philadelphia: J. P. Lippincott, 1949. Reprinted by permission.

and several hundred Mexicans milled around each of the police substations and the Central Jail trying to get word of missing members of their families. Boys came into the police stations saying: "Charge me with vagrancy or anything, but don't send me out there!" pointing to the streets where other boys, as young as twelve and thirteen years of age were being beaten and stripped of their clothes. . . .

At midnight on June seventh, the military authorities decided that the local police were completely unable or unwilling to handle the situation, despite the fact that a thousand reserve officers had been called up. The entire downtown area of Los Angeles was then declared "out of bounds" for military personnel. This order immediately slowed down the pace of the rioting. The moment the Military Police and Shore Patrol went into action, the rioting quieted down. On June eighth the city officials brought their heads up out of the sand, took a look around, and began issuing statements. The district attorney, Fred N. Howser, announced that the "situation is getting entirely out of hand," while Mayor Fletcher Bowron thought that "sooner or later it will blow over." The chief of police, taking a count of the Mexicans in jail, cheerfully proclaimed that "the situation has now cleared up." All agreed, however, that it was quite "a situation."

Unfortunately, "the situation" had not cleared up; nor did it blow over. It began to spread to the suburbs where the rioting continued for two more days. When it finally stopped, the Eagle Rock *Advertiser* mournfully editorialized: "It is too bad the servicemen were called off before they were able to complete the job. . . . Most of the citizens of the city have been delighted with what has been going on." County Supervisor Roger Jessup told the newsmen: "All that is needed to end lawlessness is more of the same action as is being exercised by the servicemen!" While the district attorney of Ventura, an outlying county, jumped on the bandwagon with a statement to the effect that "zoot-suits are an open indication of subversive character."

What Do You Think? _____

Why do things like "zoot-suits" offend people? Are there some contemporary styles that might produce the same reaction? Explain.

---

4. Drugs? Alcoholism?*

Alcohol is a mood-changing drug. Is overuse or abuse of liquor a form of self-destruction? What causes drug-abuse or alcoholism?

*Enid Nemy, "Youth and Alcohol Abuse: 'Alarming' Problem Here," *The New York Times,* August 19, 1974. Copyright © 1974 by The New York Times Company. Reprinted by permission.

Dr. Morris Chafetz, director of the National Institute on Alcohol Abuse and Alcoholism, said that 14 percent of high school seniors across the nation get drunk at least once a week. And national figures compiled by the United States Department of Health Education and Welfare indicate that by the time they are in the seventh grade 63 percent of boys and 54 percent of girls already have had at least one drink.

Allan Luks, executive director of the New York City affiliate of the National Council on Alcoholism, insisted that the problem goes beyond drinking.

"It's not an alcohol problem, it's a drug problem," he asserted. "Society is concentrating on eliminating the use of drugs like heroin, but it hasn't solved the switch to another drug to get a high.

"The dramatic use of mood-changing drugs by youth parallels the increasing stress and strains we find in urban life, the break-up of the traditional family, and the new drug laws and decreasing supplies of narcotics," he continued.

"Alcohol is cheap and legally and readily available. Youngsters don't understand it is a road to addiction that can kill. Parents don't understand the similarity of all mood-changing drugs and therefore don't worry about their children's use of alcohol."

Mr. Luks said, too, that young people now were either ingesting alcohol at a faster rate than their parents did or had an addiction problem of another kind before starting on alcohol.

The percentage of alcoholism among the young is still a small one. It is, however, Mr. Luks said, highly significant because alcholism usually requires years to develop and there are indications that it is now becoming a disease of the young, rather than the middle-aged.

"We receive about 4,500 calls a year and 2,500 of them result in referral for treatment," he said. "Before the 1970's, the number of teen-agers and young adults was almost nil. Last year, we had 24 referrals for treatment under 19 years of age, and 109 in the 20-to-25 year old category."

"Sure the number of fullblown alcoholics is still a small percentage of the total, but the number of kids drinking in the schools is an enormous problem," said John Guerin, director of Alcohol Services of the city's Department of Mental Health. "There's a major question of whether these people will become alcoholics."

10 Million Alcoholics

"There is a 50 percent probability that the child of an alcoholic might become an alcoholic," observed John Alfieri, chairman of the Committee on Youth of the National Council on Alcoholism, New York Division. He noted that there are an estimated 10 million alcoholics in the United States.

To Earl Jung, of the high school division of the Board of Education, adolescent alcohol abuse is an uphill battle "because alcohol is socially acceptable."

41

What Do You Think? _____

1. Would you consider overdrinking of alcohol a form of violence? Toward whom?
2. Is drug taking in the same class as alcoholism? Do both serve the same purpose? Explain.
3. How would you treat alcoholics, or drug addicts? As sick persons? Criminals? People free to make their own choices? Explain your answer.

---

5. Political Extremism?*

This case of violence in San Francisco, California, involved groups of people organized for political action. Why do these groups express so much dislike of each other?

A riot broke out in Nourse Auditorium last night between Nazi party members and several dozen persons attending the Board of Education meeting on integration plans for San Francisco's junior and senior high schools.

Ten persons—six men and four women were arrested.

One man was hospitalized with facial cuts suffered in the melee. He was in good condition following treatment at San Francisco General hospital.

*"Ten Arrested in Fight with Nazis," *San Francisco Chronicle,* January 9, 1974. Copyright © Chronicle Publishing Co., 1974.

More than 600 persons were in the auditorium, awaiting the start of public testimony on the controversial integration plan, when fighting erupted at 7:25 p.m.

Some 30 members of the Workers Action Movement, who had been picketing outside the auditorium, sat behind the Nazis, shouted at them, then began hitting them with fists and placards.

Within moments there were a dozen separate fights going on.

Minutes later, more than 50 policeman—many wearing riot gear—charged into the auditorium.

The Nazis quickly resumed their seats, stoically faced the front of the auditorium and kept quiet.

As WAM members and others continued to shout and attempt to strike the Nazis, the police quickly grabbed them and escorted them to the lobby. Those who resisted had to be forcibly removed.

Meanwhile, Dr. Eugene S. Hopp, president of the Board of Education, kept shouting for order and threatening to clear the auditorium.

Hardly anyone could hear him. In addition to the shouts and screams in the auditorium, the public address system went out of order, filling the huge room with an eerie whine.

The mad scene lasted about 20 minutes.

It was the most violent incident in the history of the Board of Education.

Before order was restored, there were 25 policemen in the front of the auditorium facing the audience, another dozen in the rear and at least a dozen more in the lobby.

One of the Nazis had been dragged from his seat on the aisle by five or six men and women. It was at that point that the large force of policemen rushed in.

When quiet resumed, one Nazi had a cut and bloody nose, another had a rapidly developing black eye.

At 9:20 p.m., after learning they were 96th and 97th on the list of speakers, the Nazis got up en masse and left, escorted by police.

There was a lot of shouting and heckling, but no further violence.

A man who had been standing near the Nazis said one of the non-Nazis jumped a plainclothes policeman and started hitting him and that's when the police began dragging people to the rear and making arrests.

"We don't throw the first punch," [a Nazi] said, "we never do."

The Workers Action Movement had been carrying signs that read: "Workers Action Movement Says Fight Racism in Schools."

When the battle began, some of that group's members hit Nazis with picket signs.

Last month, on December 4, a Board of Education meeting was interrupted when several black persons objected to the presence of six uniformed members of the National Socialist White People's Party, also known as the Nazi party.

[A] member of the Black Teachers Caucus then shouted, "I don't want to sit in the same room with them."

43

There was no violence last month, but when the Nazis took off their coats and revealed their swastika armbands last night, [one person] rushed to the microphone and demanded the board have the Nazis thrown out.

As she screamed, others joined in and the battle was under way.

What Do You Think? _____

1. Should Nazis or other groups opposed to the American way of life be allowed to speak at public meetings? Why or why not?
2. Who—or what—caused the violence in this incident?

---

6. "It's Terrible That Life Can Be So Cheap"*

In the following reading, the author tries to analyze the reasons for violence in one of our nation's larger cities—Detroit, Michigan. Would what he has to say about Detroit be true of other cities as well?

One day last week in Detroit, a lawyer in a Hall of Justice courtroom inexplicably drew a gun and pointed it at the judge and a witness. The judge was not carrying the .38 caliber pistol that he usually packs, but three policemen in the courtroom drew their guns and killed the lawyer. A few minutes later, in a luggage shop in downtown Detroit, the owner and his clerk were discovered neatly trussed and executed, apparently in a robbery. A little after that, a prominent black psychiatrist was found dead in the trunk of his car. And still later that evening, police in the suburb of Roseville came across the bodies of a pair of young lovers in a car, victims of a murder-suicide.

Since Jan. 1, there have been 187 homicides in Detroit, 27 percent ahead of the rate last year in the city that normally revels in records. Last year Detroit (pop. 1.5 million) had 601 homicides, or one for every 2,500 people. By contrast, Chicago, with twice as many people, had 711 murders; while London (pop. 7.4 million) had only 113.

Why is Detroit such a center for bloodletting? Police Commissioner John Nichols believes that the widespread possession of handguns is a basic cause. He estimates that there are some 500,000 handguns around, or one for every three citizens of Detroit. Nichols is backed by the studies of Dr. Emanuel Tanay, a professor of psychiatry and law at Wayne State University, who says that "Detroit is almost like an experiment in testing the correlation between the presence of guns and homicide." Tanay notes that over a period of six years, the number of gun permits tripled and the rate of homicides by firearms increased eightfold; in the same period, homicide by any other means rose by only 50 percent.

*"Murder City," *Time,* April 1973. Reprinted by permission from TIME, The Weekly News Magazine. Copyright Time Inc.

Police say that the surge in ownership of guns—most of them unregistered —started after blacks burned and sacked large parts of the city's ghetto areas in the 1967 riots. "It seemed like everybody went out and bought a gun," one officer recalls. Now that so many guns are handy, the argument over the kitchen table at 2 a.m., which might once have ended in a punch in the nose, has a good chance of ending with a bullet in the gut. The police log offers these samples: an argument in the Red Dog Bar, a disagreement in Cherry's Poolroom, a quarrel over the whereabouts of the money from the welfare check, an argument over rent. Narcotics were involved in 10 percent to 12 percent of the homicides; most of the victims and the murderers were black; one-third of the crimes remain unsolved. The majority of the murders continue to be the work of friends or relatives of the victims. Of 111 homicides in February, 72 occurred inside the home. And guns are used about 60 percent of the time.

The high homicide rate is a cultural problem as well as a gun problem. Detroit's need for unskilled labor has brought in vast numbers of rural Southern blacks and increasing numbers of rural whites. Says Homicide Inspector John Domm: "The kids grow up in a culture of aggression, the poor and the black learn to get ahead by being aggressive. People who look for the police to solve this problem are looking in the wrong direction." Meanwhile, Dr. Tanay warns that the chances of getting murdered in a gun-laden society are so great that it is unwise even to argue with a stranger during, say, a traffic mishap.

What Do You Think?

1. "The city (Detroit) is a monument to urban sickness." What does this mean? Would this be true of other cities as well?

2. The author suggests that one reason there may be more violence in Detroit than in any other American city is because Detroit is a factory city. Would being a factory city contribute to violence? Why or why not?

3. What does the author mean by saying Detroit has a "cultural problem as well as a gun problem"? Which do you think of as a more serious cause of crime and other forms of violence?

7. The Wish for Death*

When we think of violence, we usually picture people hurting others. But what about people who harm themselves? Might a wish to harm oneself be a cause of violence?

This year, if recent history is any indication, at least 25,000 Americans will kill themselves. No one will ever be able to do more than guess at how

*"Suicide Among the Young Rises Sharply," *Long Island Press*, 1974.

many attempt suicide and fail, but educated guesses put the figure at about 250,000 annually.

These figures, grim though they may seem, have held fairly constant over the past decade, and suicide rates in this country are actually lower today than they were earlier in the century. But within the overall statistics there has been a reshuffling: astonishingly, rates among older men and women are dropping and youthful suicides . . . predominantly in the 15 to 24 age bracket . . . are showing a disturbing increase.

Cause-of-death statistics compiled by the government place suicide in the top five among the 15 to 24 year olds, along with accidents, cancer, heart and kidney disease and murder. And many experts think suicide belongs in the number two position, right after accidents.

Thousands of "accidental deaths," they say, aren't accidental at all; they are suicides that families report as accidents to avoid the stigma attached to self-inflicted deaths. For suicide is one of our most enduring taboos.

This shame attached to suicide is one reason why suicide statistics are at best only good estimates. Another reason: many insurance programs penalize the beneficiaries of suicide victims . . . another excuse for families to hush up the true story.

Many specialists began studying the numbers, the psychology and the sociology of suicide. They called their discipline, suicidology.

Few were prepared for what they found. Historically, suicide rates increased with advancing age . . . people got older, the reasoning went, and they encountered crippling diseases or severe hardships, or they despaired over life-goals unattained. Yet in the 1950s and 1960s, young people began killing themselves at a faster and faster rate. And that rate is still growing.

Men and women in the 45 to 54 age group, for example, have been taking their own lives at the reported rate of about 20 per 100,000 for 30 years. The number of reported suicides per 100,000 young people from 15 to 24, however, has gone from 4.3 in 1944 to 6.0 in 1963 to 8.0 in 1969 to 9.7 in 1972. Thus, youthful suicides are still far less frequent than suicides among older people, but the rate is increasing alarmingly.

"There definitely has been a dramatic drop in the age level of suicides," says Dr. Richard H. Seiden, a University of California professor who has done several studies of suicide attempts, "and it's a nationwide trend."

Adds Dr. Herbert Hendin, a Columbia University psychiatrist who has just completed a three-year study of suicide among college students: "It's not really surprising that more and more young people are going to suicide. Everything is moving down in age: drugs, sex . . . so why not suicide?"

No one boasts of knowing just why the rate is climbing among the young. There are too many unanswered questions. But Dr. Seiden does offer a suggestion.

"If you break down the suicide figures by race or ethnic group," he says, "you find that the really big increase for young people is with blacks and Chicanos. While among white suicides rates still climb into middle age and beyond, the minority groups seem to reach their peak in the early years . . . the 20's and 30's. It's just guesswork, but it seems that a typical white suicide realizes that he's not going to reach his goals sometime in the later years; for minority groups that realization is coming earlier."

Traditionally, it was thought that the middle-class was more suicide-prone than the poor; poor people, went the reasoning, didn't expect much out of life, so they had little to be disappointed about. But recent civil rights gains appear to have brought about increased expectations among poor non-whites. When these new aspirations prove unrealistic, despair sets in.

It seems to be the young, especially, who become quickly disillusioned.

But such disappointments account for only some of the total number of suicides, young and old. The reasons why people take their own lives are many, and often are hidden forever. Only 15 or 20 percent of suicide victims leave explanatory notes; young suicides rarely do.

But "psychological autopsies," based on interviews with surviving family members and close friends of suicide victims, have provided some hints. "The common denominator," says one expert, "seems to be an awful loneliness and isolation."

What Do You Think? _____

1. What does this author think are the major causes of suicide for all people? For youths?
2. Which of the causes of suicide do you believe are most important? Why?

---

8. Movies

It seems that people are always willing to pay good prices at the box office to see blood, gore, and conflict. Are these films a subtle influence in fostering violence, or simply a reminder of the values we already hold?

Scenes from Hollywood movies.

1. Are these movies glorifying violence?
2. Why do movies frequently display violent behavior to mass audiences?
3. Do violent movies make people violent, or do violent people make violent movies?
4. Would you agree or disagree with the idea that "brutal and savage films bring about violence"?
5. Or would you agree with the idea that "violent films symbolize the conflict we all find enjoyable"?
6. Do violent movies harm people psychologically? Do they make them more prone to violence? Explain your reasoning.

---

9. Our Aggressive Tendencies*

In 1932, as a part of a League of Nations study on war, Sigmund Freud and Albert Einstein exchanged letters examining the causes of human aggression. Both sought to explain conflict and to find the ways of lessening it. In his answer to Einstein, Freud presented his view of the origins of human violence, and his opinion about eliminating it. A few passages from that letter are reproduced below. Would you agree with Freud?

Conflicts of interest between man and man are resolved, in principle, by the recourse to violence. It is the same in the animal kingdom, from which man cannot claim exclusion; nevertheless men are also prone to conflicts of opinion, touching, on occasion, the loftiest peaks of abstract thought, which seems to call for settlement by quite another method. This refinement is, however, a late development. To start with, brute force was the factor which, in small communities, decided points of ownership and the question of which man's will was to prevail. Very soon physical force was implemented, then replaced, by the use of various adjuncts; he proved the victor whose weapon was the better, or handled the more skillfully. Now, for the first time, with the coming of weapons, superior brains began to oust brute force, but the object of the conflict remained the same: one party was to be constrained, by the injury done him or impairment of his strength, to retract a claim or a refusal. This end is most effectively gained when the opponent is definitively put out of action—in other words, is killed. This procedure has two advantages; the enemy cannot renew hostilities, and, secondly, his fate deters others from following his example.

*Excerpted from "Why War?" League of Nations International Institute of Intellectual Cooperation, Paris, France, 1933.

Moreover, the slaughter of a foe gratifies an instinctive craving—a point to which we shall revert hereafter. However, another consideration may be set off against this will to kill: the possibility of using an enemy for servile tasks if his spirit be broken and his life spared. Here violence finds an outlet not in slaughter but in subjugation. Hence springs the practice of giving quarter; but the victor, having from now on to reckon with the craving for revenge that rankles in his victim, forfeits to some extent his personal security.

Thus, under primitive conditions, it is superior force—brute violence, or violence backed by arms—that lords it everywhere. We know that in the course of evolution this state of things was modified, a path was traced that led away from violence to law. But what was this path? Surely it issued from a single verity; that the superiority of one strong man can be overborne by an alliance of many weaklings, that "l'union fait la force." Brute force is overcome by union, the allied might of scattered units makes good its right against the isolated giant. Thus we may define "right" (i.e. law) as the might of a community. Yet it, too, is nothing else than violence, quick to attack whatever individual stands in its path, and it employs the selfsame methods, follows like end, with but one difference; it is the communal, not individual, violence that has its way. But, for the transition from crude violence to the reign of law, a certain psychological condition must first obtain. The union of the majority must be stable and enduring. If its sole "raison d'etre" be the discomfiture of some overweening individual and, after his downfall, it be dissolved, it leads to nothing. Some other man, trusting to his superior power, will seek to reinstate the rule of violence and the cycle will repeat itself unendingly. Thus the union of the people must be permanent and well organized; it must enact rules to meet the risk of possible revolts; must set up machinery ensuring that its rules —the laws—are observed and that such acts of violence as the laws demand are duly carried out. This recognition of a community of interests engenders among the members of the group a sentiment of unity and fraternal solidarity which constitutes its real strength. . . . (Thus it would seem that any effort to replace brute force by the might of an ideal is, under present conditions, doomed to fail. Our logic is at fault if we ignore the fact that right is founded on brute force and even today needs violence to maintain it.)

I now can comment on another of your statements. You are amazed that it is so easy to infect men with the war-fever, and you surmise that man has in him an active instinct for hatred and destruction, amenable to such stimulations. I entirely agree with you. I believe in the existence of this instinct and have been recently at pains to study its manifestations. . . .

The upshot of these observations, as bearing on the subject in hand, is that there is no likelihood of our being able to suppress humanity's aggressive tendencies. In some happy corners of the earth, they say, where nature brings forth abundantly whatever man desires, there flourish races whose lives go gently by, unknowing of aggression or constraint. This I can hardly credit; I would like further details about these happy folk. . . . In any case, as you too have observed, complete suppression of man's aggressive tendencies is not in issues; what we may try is to divert it into a channel other than that of warfare.

What Do You Think?

1. What explanation does Freud offer for violent behavior? Can you find cases that support his theory? Refute it?
2. According to Freud's ideas, is it possible for people to lessen their violent tendencies? Why or why not?
3. What would you say, at this point, to be the major causes of violence? Explain.

10. TV Violence

A study by Drs. Paul Ekman, Robert Liebert, Wallace Friesen, and others of the Department of Psychiatry at the University of California, San Francisco, reports that five- and six-year-old boys who seemed pleased while viewing violence on television were later aggressive toward parents and peers. By contrast, youngsters who seemed upset or indifferent to the violence portrayed later proved to be more helpful to people. Is TV violence a cause or symptom of our society's values and behavior?

Drawing by Stees. Los Angeles Times Syndicate.

Drawing by Liederman. ROTHCO.

What Do You Think?

1. What points are being made by these two cartoons? Would you agree with either of them? Why or why not?

2. How does the summary of a research report on viewing TV violence relate to the cartoons? To what extent does this report support or undermine the idea that watching violence on TV breeds "real" violence?

ACTIVITIES FOR INVOLVEMENT

1. Interview a random sample of people to see if they would agree or disagree with the following statements. How would you explain your findings?
   a. Humanity is inherently violent and always will be.
   b. In a perfect state, with a fair and just system of laws and government, violence would fade away.
   c. Violence is taught by parents to their children.
   d. As poverty increases, so does violence; and as poverty decreases, so does violence.

2. Some social scientists claim that violent behavior arises out of conflicts of interest or conflicts of value. Conflicts of interest arise when two or more parties want the same goods, wealth, or position. Conflicts of value arise when two or more parties from the same social group, society or nation view different things as good or worthy. Review all the examples in this chapter and indicate which ones fit the two rules given above and which do not fit. See if you can find any additional examples that have happened in the last month that support or refute this theory of conflict due to different interests or different values.

3. The causes of violence have been discussed a great deal throughout history. Two major theories of violence have long been popular. One says that people are violent because they have inherited the instinct for it—it is part of human biology. The second theory holds that social conditions create violence—that it is learned by example, from teachers, parents, and other adults. Do some research to find out where a few famous thinkers stand on this issue. Look through the writings of Aristotle, Machiavelli, Charles Darwin, and Karl Marx and estimate which theory they would support. Add any other authors you wish to your study.

4. Take a poll to discover what a random sampling of people in various groups believe causes violence. Make up a series of questions that give your respondents a choice of causes and a choice of responses (ranging from strongly disagree, disagree, don't know, agree, to strongly agree). Conduct polls for different groups, for instance: (a) your neighbors, (b) your friends, (c) your classmates, (d) students at a local university, (e) police, and (f) politicians. Compare the results of your polling. What differences do you note in these findings? How would you explain these differences?

5. Look up the examples of American violence listed below in an American history book or other source. Classify each example according to what seems to be the major reason for the violence. Count the number of times violence occurred for any one reason. Make a chart of the count. Which reason seems to explain most adequately in your opinion the largest number of violent events?
   a. Bacon's Rebellion (1676)
   b. Boston Massacre (1770)
   c. Whiskey Rebellion (1794)
   d. Harpers Ferry (1859)
   e. Railroad Strike (1870)
   f. Pullman Strike (1894)
   g. Ludlow, Colorado (1913–1914)
   h. Chicago Eviction Riot (1931)
   i. Vessey Uprising (1822)
   j. New York Draft Riot (1863)
   k. Detroit Riot (1943)

l. Watts (1965)

m. Wounded Knee Massacre (1890)

n. Anti-Mormon Riot (1838)

o. Bonus Army (1932)

p. Freedom Riders (1961)

q. Hamilton-Burr Duel (1804)

r. Gunfight at the O.K. Corral (1881)

s. Assassination of Lincoln (1865)

t. Murder of Malcolm X (1965)

u. San Francisco Vigilante Committee (1865)

v. Attica Prison Revolt (1971)

w. Kidnapping of Patricia Hearst (1974)

6. Invite a psychiatrist as a guest speaker. Ask him to explain what he thinks are the causes of violent behavior, both underlying and immediate. Compare his theory of violence with some of those expressed in this chapter. Have a classroom discussion in which you discuss which cause or group of causes are the most important reasons for violence, which the least important, and why.

7. Many people believe that the police, rather than keeping the peace, often provoke violence themselves. Find out and report to the class what you can do about cases of police brutality, harassment, or illegal procedures. What solutions would you suggest to this problem? What solutions would other class members suggest? How do your suggestions compare with those to be found in a booklet published by the Civil Liberties Union entitled "Police Complaints"? Which of the ideas suggested might work? Why? Invite a lawyer from the American Civil Liberties Union to speak to the class about his experiences in handling suits and complaints against the police, and a police officer to explain departmental procedures for dealing with complaints against police officers. Which procedures seem most effective? Why?

8. Under what conditions are people nonviolent? Set up a debate over the proposition that, "in a just and equal society, people will have no need to engage in violence to fill their needs or express their anger and hatred." Justice may be defined as fair and impartial treatment under the law for all people, regardless of race, creed, sex, color, or national origin; while equality may be defined as equal treatment under the law and a relatively fair share of society's goods and services.

5
WHAT ARE THE EFFECTS OF VIOLENCE?

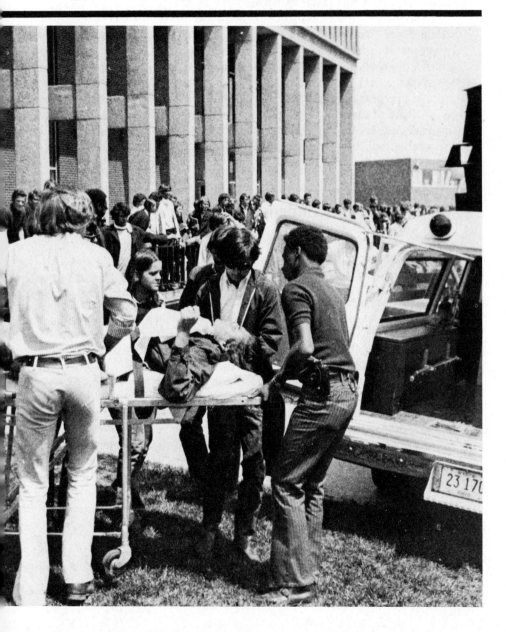

At one and the same time, people may feel excited by violence yet also fearful of it. Many Americans seem to enjoy violence—at least they seem to enjoy reading and hearing about it. But the vast majority prefer to be far away from any real harm. When violence does occur, the desire for safety, protection, and "law and order" grows and grows rapidly.

As you read in Chapter 2, fascination with violence is not something new. Past societies have also been interested in conflict and have very often glorified it. Warrior cults and hero worship are very ancient. Even bandits have been raised at times to the status of heroes.

This abiding appreciation of violence, however, is matched by an equally strong desire of people to live secure and peaceful lives. In situations where people become fearful for their safety and the safety of their belongings, violence becomes a social issue of great importance.

What effects do the various forms of violence have on people—their attitudes, personalities, and desires? What effects does violence have on society itself? Some of the effects of violence, such as death, devastation, and great financial cost, are obvious. But there are other costs as well. The readings in this chapter will help you come to some conclusions about the dangers and results of violence.

1. A Decline in Confidence*

Worrying about crime seems to sap public confidence in law enforcement agencies. Many people want "law and order" as a result. How do you feel?

Compared with three years ago, public confidence in the performance of law enforcement officials at all levels—federal, state, and local—has dipped sharply. The decline in the standing of federal law enforcement agencies has been most dramatic: in 1973, they receive a 47–42 percent negative rating, compared to 60–30 percent positive in 1970.

Behind this fall-off in confidence in policing efforts across the country is the conviction now on the part of 69 percent of the public that "our system of law enforcement does not discourage people from committing crimes." Back in 1967, 56 percent shared that view.

At the same time, while the number of Americans who report that crime is increasing in the area where they live comes to a substantial 48 percent, this is down sharply from the 62 percent who reported crime on the rise in their own neighborhoods in 1970. Paradoxically, there appears to be some lessening of public apprehension over local crime concurrent with a more critical appraisal of law enforcement agencies.

*The Harris Survey, Public Confidence in Law Enforcement Has Declined, October 1973. Reprinted by permission of the Chicago Tribune. Copyright © 1973. All rights reserved.

Basically, these results could be interpreted to mean that the so-called "law-and-order" issue, claimed by some to be the dominant force in the country affecting policies and government, is beginning to be viewed in a much different light than previously. It might be considerably more difficult in the future to rally an emotional public response around such slogans as "back up your local police." Rather, people will more likely be examining more closely the actual effectiveness of law enforcement efforts as they work out in practice.

Recently, the Harris Survey asked a nationwide cross section of the public, as it had done in 1970:

"How would you rate the job done by law enforcement officials on (READ LIST) level—excellent, pretty good, only fair, or poor?"

Ratings of Local, State, and Federal Law Enforcement Officials

	Good-Excellent	Only Fair-Poor	Not Sure
Local Law Enforcement Officials			
1973	58%	39%	3%
1970	64%	33%	3%
State Law Enforcement Officials			
1973	51%	40%	9%
1970	63%	30%	7%
Federal Law Enforcement Officials			
1973	42%	47%	11%
1970	60%	30%	10%

While public confidence in law enforcement officials has been declining, so has the crime rate perceived by residents in their own areas.

The public was asked:

"In the past year, do you feel the crime rate in your area has been increasing, decreasing, or has it remained the same as it was before?"

Crime Rate in Own Area

	1973	1970	1967
Increasing	48%	62%	46%
Decreasing	7%	3%	4%
Remained same	40%	30%	43%
Not sure	5%	5%	7%

Significantly, the one area of the country where crime is reported by local residents to be increasing is the South, where 55 percent of the people say it is on the rise. To a surprising degree, Southerners also are more critical of their own local law enforcement officials than residents in any other part of the country.

A major objective of law enforcement, most people believe, is to discour-

57

age crimes from being committed. It is precisely in this function that people feel that law enforcement agencies are failing. In several surveys, the Harris Survey has asked cross sections of the public:

"From what you know or have heard, do you feel that our system of law enforcement works to really discourage people from committing crimes, or don't you feel it discourages them much?"

Does Law Enforcement System Really Discourage Crime?

	1973	1970	1967
Really discourages crime	18%	18%	26%
Doesn't discourage crime much	69%	67%	56%
Encourages crime (vol.)	4%	4%	6%
Not sure	9%	11%	12%

Crime prevention is an area receiving increasing public attention. The probability is that it will become the target of many searching questions directed toward police agencies at the federal, state, and local levels. For now it is apparent that law enforcement agencies, so long immune from public criticism, are going to be put on their mettle by the people themselves.

What Do You Think?

1. Is criminal violence here to stay?
2. What effect might such a belief have on hope, trust, and public confidence in the legal system?

2. Anger*

What does this incident suggest about the effects of violence?

The other day I had occasion to pull down from my bookshelf the "Report of the National Advisory Commission on Civil Disorders." It was published just five years ago, but already it sounds with the distant ring of history. The symbol of our troubled times is Watergate. It is no longer Watts.

How strange and out-of-date they seem, the "profiles of disorder" which open the book—Cincinnati, Atlanta, Newark, Detroit. Police brutality. Snipers. Burn, baby, burn. National Guard. Rage.

I suppose life is more civilized since we moved on to impeachment and inflation and energy. We still hear occasionally from Roy Wilkins and Ron Dellums. But the race crisis—which we all agreed in the 1960's was the great unresolved question in our national destiny—seems almost to have vanished.

But has it? The Kerner Commission, you remember, warned us starkly: "Our nation is moving toward two societies, one black, one white—separate and unequal." The blacks of the period, especially the young, complained specifically of inferior education, lack of employment opportunities, poor housing. Has it become any better for them?

I suppose there have been some ups and some downs. We, as a nation, have tried hard to integrate our schools, but it's not clear we've succeeded in improving education. We've surely widened job opportunities for qualified blacks, but black unemployment remains disproportionately high. As for housing, it's measurably worse than five years ago.

But, still, the ghettos are quiet—even if no one understands quite why. Was rioting just a fad, which ran its course?

But a more important question than why riots happened in the 1960's, or stopped in the 1970's, is whether they could happen again in the 1980's, or before. The ominous theme of the Kerner Report is that they could.

I wondered, in fact, whether that was the meaning of a small incident that occurred not long ago when I was driving with a French journalist, showing him our city.

He hadn't expected, he said, to see blacks and whites shopping together, eating side by side in restaurants, weaving easily past one another on crowded sidewalks. He was amazed, he said, to see how many blacks worked with whites in government offices.

I confirmed the accuracy of his findings and said that, had he visited ten years ago, it would not have been that way. But I admonished him against oversimplifying—and said there still was considerable tension in the air.

It was only a few minutes later that I pulled up for a red light behind a car on a main thoroughfare, and my friend spied something off to the left he wanted to see. So I slowly turned the steering wheel to pull off into the adjoining land and, in so doing, lightly tapped the car's rear bumper.

As my car came abreast, I looked over and saw three black faces staring furiously at me. I apologized profusely for my clumsiness, far more humbly than circumstances might otherwise have demanded. Then a man got out of the car and slowly strode back to examine the bumper, microscopically it seemed to me until he was satisfied no damage had been done.

As we drove away, with some bemusement, mixed into my feelings of relief, I said to the Frenchman, "You see what I mean about tension?" We both laughed, a little tightly, and he said, "I see what you mean."

It wasn't much of an incident, over in a few minutes. But it contained fierce anger, and it seemed to say that we mustn't be fooled by the tranquility of our times.

59

Does anger and resentment necessarily lead to violence? Why or why not?

3. Bitterness*

Historical patterns and relationships between conquered and conquerers often sow the seeds of hate and conflict for centuries. Is this true of Indian–white relations in the United States today?

The city of Farmington is beginning to reap a crop of bitterness.

The seed was sown a hundred years ago, when invading white settlers started moving up the frozen San Juan River into a lovely green valley favored as a wintering spot by gold prospectors.

It has been brought to flower by oil and gas and alcohol.

And now, spurred by the senseless murder of three drunken men and by growing resentment of the casual discrimination that has long set Indians apart from whites in the Southwest, the once placid Navajo Indians are demanding redress.

The whole thing has come as somewhat of a surprise to Farmington; but then it would be rare for anyone caught up in the unfolding of a history as long and intense as this one to realize it at the time.

Helen Foultz, the daughter of a one-time Farmington Mayor, wrote in 1951 about the beginning:

"It seems that great-grandfather Foultz was traveling this way with his two good wives, Aunt Emma and Aunt Susan, in their covered wagon.

"The Indians were on the warpath and troubling them considerable. When they entered this valley, they found themselves completely surrounded by them."

"Great-grandfather made his decision. We'll just stay here until we outnumber them," he said.

"That explains why there are so many Foultzes. . . ."

Her great-grandfather was a Mormon, as were most of the first whites to settle this area. There were many Indians—Utes, Apaches and the beleaguered Navajo, who had been driven from pillar to post and finally settled forcibly in eastern Arizona and western New Mexico in 1868 after their defeat by Col. Kit Carson.

The Indians posed no legal problem to the Mormons. The Hopi were the

*Martin Waldron, "Farmington, N.M., Is Beginning to Harvest Fruits of 100 Years of Indian Bitterness and Frustration," *The New York Times,* July 6, 1974. Copyright © 1974 by The New York Times Company. Reprinted by permission.

An assistant U.S. Attorney General is led by armed members of the American Indian Movement to confer with their leaders who took over the village of Wounded Knee, South Dakota, for several weeks.

only American Indians with a strong attachment to a particular piece of land. Other Indians had no conception of individual ownership of land, treating the earth as being owned in common by all living men.

A hundred years ago, the San Juan River Basin was the only livable area in the four corners area of New Mexico. The mile-high mesas did not get enough rain to grow sufficient grass to attract buffalo. The melting snow in the 13,000-foot-high Rocky Mountains 100 miles to the north kept the San Juan River flowing all year long.

Many were also violence-prone, like Dobey Jack, who sucked raw eggs from the shell for his lunch and who "took to drinking" after accidentally causing his wife's death by shooting her through the head.

The white pioneers tolerated neither marauding Indians nor the white outlaws who began to raid the river settlements. The farmers and merchants formed vigilante groups to dispense arbitrary frontier justice.

They thought of the Navajo, whose reservation abutted the valley, as worthless savages at best.

It had been known for years that oil and gas lay under the dry, dusty mesas around Farmington, but the land was harsh outside the valley and there was no real effort to do anything about it until the El Paso Natural Gas Company built a 24-inch gas line from Farmington to California in 1951.   **61**

By 1956, after the Pacific Northwest Gas Company's line to Seattle had opened, outsiders flocked into Farmington and turned it into an oil and gas town.

By 1958, Farmington's population had soared to 30,000, and more than $1 billion in outside money had been invested in the area. The little town had become a little city.

The oil and gas workers who now overran Farmington worked hard and drank hard, and paid no attention to the growing alienation of the Indians.

The Navajos, once so destitute that many were in danger of starving, were becoming more affluent. In 1953, the state's prohibition against selling alcohol to Indians was struck down, and the Navajos, who once had to depend on bootleggers for whiskey, began to patronize saloons openly. Drunken Indians sleeping on the streets became a police problem.

Sociologists have offered various explanations for the seeming Indian predilection for overindulgence in alcohol: frustration, unemployment, feelings of inferiority engendered by official and unofficial discrimination.

Stories are told that in Farmington, high school youths made a game out of "rolling" drunken Indians who were sleeping off binges in an alley or a gutter.

In recent years, the best pickings have been near the "Indian" bars that sprang up on Highway 550 west of Farmington.

In April of this year, the bodies of three Navajo men were found in small canyons on the mesas north of Farmington. The three men were 34, 39, and 52 years of age. All lived in the area.

They had been beaten to death, their heads or bodies crushed by rocks. Rumors spread that the bodies had been mutilated with knives.

All three men were reported to have been murdered while drunk.

They were not the first Indians to die from violence in the area. It has become almost commonplace for Indians to be killed while drunk. Many have died in car wrecks, others in fights. Some have attacked the police and have been killed while being subdued.

A number of young Navajos, intent on focusing attention on dual problems—discrimination and Indian alcoholism—seized on the murders to rally support for demonstrations in Farmington.

Shortly after they began their weekend marches through the towns, where they pressed their demands that "Indian" bars be closed as public nuisances, the police arrested three white Farmington teen-agers who confessed to killing the Indians. Two of the boys were 16 years old, one was 15.

After undergoing psychiatric examinations, the three white youths were taken before state District Judge Frank Zinn for a hearing to decide whether they should be tried as adults.

Judge Zinn is from Gallup, a city 120 miles south of here that has had its share of Indian violence and demonstrations in recent years.

The hearing was closed. It was announced afterward that Judge Zinn had given the three boys an indeterminate sentence in a state correctional institution for juvenile defendants.

The demonstrating Navajos continued to protest, although they did not make the sentences given the three teen-agers an issue. They continued to demand that the Indian bars be closed.

A demonstration scheduled for one weekend was canceled as a gesture of respect to the families of three other Indian men—two Zunis and a Navajo—who were found stabbed to death in June near Gallup. The police said these three Indians had apparently been killed by other Indians.

Investigators have not yet found who beat to death and mutilated three other Navajos near Gallup a year ago.

The National Indian Youth Council, an Albuquerque-based Indian Civil rights group, has asked the Justice Department to determine whether there is a pattern to the series of murders.

Gerald Wilkinson, the executive director of the council, says there is a suggestion of "a conspiracy to kill Indian people in connection with a ritualistic racism."

The situation has created a good bit of emotion in Farmington. Many of the old-line whites want the city to adopt a law-and-order stance and refuse to compromise with the Indians. Letter after letter to the local newspaper has the same theme: "No one forces the Indians to drink," and "Indians don't deserve special consideration."

Mayor Marlo Webb, after some weeks of waiting, has appointed a "Navajo relations committee" to recommend ways to eliminate any discrimination toward Indians in Farmington.

Fred E. Johnson, a Navajo attorney, and another demonstration leader, Larry Emerson, were named to the committee.

The Navajo tribal council also has appointed a Navajo civil rights commission to hear complaints from Indians about discrimination.

But thus far, the angry young Navajos who have been leading the demonstrations seem unconvinced that the pattern of a hundred years of neglect and discrimination has been broken. And they promise to continue agitation.

What Do You Think? _____

1. How has history molded life in Farmington, New Mexico?
2. What is probably the underlying reason for Indian "bitterness and frustration?" Do other minority groups have the same feelings? If so, which ones and why? If not, why not?

4. Prison Revolts

Many people believe that prisons are supposed to rehabilitate criminals. Others feel prisons were designed for punishment. Whatever the rationale, prisons often seem   **63** *to heighten violence and brutality, making inmates more dangerous than they were before. Do you believe prisons lessen or heighten discontent and hatred?*

Some of the negotiators representing rebelling prisoners at Attica prison.

State police herding subdued inmates after the Attica rebellion.

1. Do prisons often breed new violence? Is the fault that of the prisoners only? The system? Or both?

2. Are hostages' lives worth the prevention of inmates' escapes?

3. Should the system be changed—made more repressive or more rehabilitative? Or left the same? Explain your reasoning.

---

5. The Glorification of Violence

Comic books, in a sense, are a literary and art form that appeals to large numbers of Americans, especially the young. What happens if such books contain large amounts of gore and conflict?

1. How do comic strip scenes, such as the one shown here, affect you?
2. A comic strip artist has said, "We have to resort to violence to protect ourselves from evil." How might you reply to this statement? How would Mr. Hofstadter (Reading 6 in this chapter) react?
3. Do comic strips showing violence promote violence? Why or why not? Could such strips promote nonviolence and peaceful values?

6. America as a Gun Culture*

Americans, seemingly more so than other people, love guns. Guns are cheap and quite easy to obtain in the United States. In this reading, a noted historian discusses the American's love of guns.

Senator Joseph Tydings of Maryland, appealing in the summer of 1968 for an effective gun-control law, lamented: "It is just tragic that in all of Western civilization the United States is the one country with an insane gun policy." In one respect this was an understatement: Western or otherwise, the United States is the only modern industrial urban nation that persists in maintaining a gun culture. It is the only industrial nation in which the possession of rifles, shotguns, and handguns is lawfully prevalent among large numbers of its population. It is the only such nation that has been impelled in recent years to agonize at length about its own disposition toward violence and to set up a commission to examine it, the only nation so attached to the supposed "right" to bear arms that its laws abet assassins, professional criminals, berserk murderers, and political terrorists at the expense of the orderly population— and yet it remains, and is apparently determined to remain, the most passive of all the major countries in the matter of gun control. Many otherwise intelligent Americans cling with pathetic stubbornness to the notion that the people's right to bear arms is the greatest protection of their individual rights and a firm safeguard of democracy—without being in the slightest perturbed by the fact that no other democracy in the world observes any such "right" and that in some democracies in which citizens' rights are rather better protected than in ours, such as England and the Scandinavian countries, our arms control policies would be considered laughable.

Laughable, however, they are not, when one begins to contemplate the costs. Since strict gun controls clearly could not entirely prevent homicides, suicides, armed robberies, or gun accidents, there is no simple way of estimating the direct human cost, much less the important indirect political costs, of having lax gun laws. But a somewhat incomplete total of firearms fatalities in the United States as of 1964 shows that in the twentieth century alone we have suffered more than 740,000 deaths from firearms, embracing over 265,000 homicides, over 330,000 suicides, and over 139,000 gun accidents. This figure is considerably higher than all the battle deaths (that is, deaths sustained under arms but excluding those from disease) suffered by American forces in all the wars in our history. It can, of course, be argued that such fatalities have been brought about less by the prevalence of guns than by some intangible factor, such as the wildness and carelessness of the American national temperament, or by particular social problems, such as the intensity of our ethnic and racial mixture. But such arguments cut both ways, since it can be held that a nation with such a temperament or such social problems needs stricter, not looser, gun controls.

One can only make a rough guess at the price Americans pay for their inability to arrive at satisfactory controls for guns. But it can be suggested in this way: there are several American cities that annually have more gun murders than all of England and Wales. In Britain, where no one may carry a firearm at night, where anyone who wants a long gun for hunting must get a certificate from the local police chief before he can buy it, and where gun dealers must verify a buyer's certificate, register all transactions in guns and ammunition, and take the serial number of each weapon and report it to the police, there are annually about .05 gun homicides per 100,000 population. In the United States there are 2.7. What this means in actual casualties may be suggested by the figures for 1963, when there were 5,126 gun murders in the United States, twenty-four in England and Wales, and three in Scotland. This

country shows up about as badly in comparative gun accidents and, to a lesser degree, in suicides. There is not a single major country in the world that approaches our record in this respect. . . .

In 1968, after the assassinations of Robert F. Kennedy and Martin Luther King, Jr., there was an almost touching national revulsion against our own gun culture, and for once the protesting correspondence on the subject reaching senators and representatives outweighed letters stirred up by the extraordinarily efficient lobby of the National Rifle Association. And yet all that came out of this moment of acute concern was a feeble measure, immensely disappointing to advocates of serious gun control, restricting the mail-order sales of guns. It seems clear now that the strategic moment for gun controls has passed and that the United States will continue to endure an armed populace,[1] at least until there is a major political disaster involving the use of guns.

Today the *urban* population of the nation is probably more heavily armed than at any time in history, largely because the close of World War II left the participating countries with a hugh surplus of militarily obsolescent but still quite usable guns. These could be sold nowhere in the world but in the United States, since no other country large enough and wealthy enough to provide a good market would have them. More weapons became available again in the 1950's, when NATO forces switched to a uniform cartridge and abandoned a stock of outmoded rifles. These again flooded the the United States, including about 100,000 Italian Carcanos of the type with which John F. Kennedy was killed. Imported very cheaply, sometimes at less than a dollar apiece, these weapons could be sold at enormous profit but still inexpensively—the one that killed Kennedy cost $12.78.

It has been estimated that between five and seven million foreign weapons were imported into the United States between 1959 and 1963. Between 1965 and 1968 handgun imports rose from 346,000 to 1,155,000. Domestic industries that make cheap handguns are approaching an annual production of 500,000 pistols a year. Thus a nation in the midst of a serious political crisis, which has frequently provoked violence, is afloat with weapons—perhaps as many as fifty million of them—in civilian hands. An Opinion Research poll of September, 1968, showed that 34 percent of a national sample of white families and 24 percent of blacks admitted to having guns. With groups like the Black Panthers and right-wing cranks like the Minute Men, not to speak of numerous white vigilante groups, well armed for trouble, the United States finds itself in a situation faced by no other Western nation. . . .

Why is the gun still so prevalent in a culture in which only about 4 percent of the country's workers now make their living from farming, a culture that for the last century and a half has had only a tiny fragment of its population actually in contact with a frontier, that, in fact, has not known a true frontier for three generations? Why did the United States alone among industrial societies cling to the idea that a substantially unregulated supply of guns

[1]Despite the attempted assassination of Governor George Wallace of Alabama in 1972.

among its city population is a safe and acceptable thing? This is, after all, not the only nation with a frontier history. Canada and Australia have had theirs, and yet their gun control measures are far more satisfactory than ours. Their own gun homicide rates, as compared with our 2.7, range around .56 and their gun suicide and accident rates are also much lower. Again, Japan, with no frontier but with an ancient tradition of feudal and military violence, has adopted, along with its modernization, such rigorous gun laws that its gun homicide rate at .04 is one of the world's lowest. (The land of hara-kiri also has one of the lowest gun suicide rates—about one fiftieth of ours.) In sum, other societies, in the course of industrial and urban development, have succeeded in modifying their old gun habits, and we have not. . . .

While the notion that "the right to bear arms" is inconsistent with state or federal gun regulation is largely confined to the obstinate lobbyists of the National Rifle Association, another belief of American gun enthusiasts enjoys a very wide currency in the United States, extending to a good many liberals, civil libertarians, and even radicals. It is the idea that popular access to arms is an important counterpoise to tyranny. A historian, recently remonstrating against our gun policies, was asked by a sympathetic liberal listener whether it was not true, for example, that one of the first acts of the Nazis had been to make it impossible for the nonparty, nonmilitary citizen to have a gun— the assumption being that the German people had thus lost their last barrier to tyranny. In fact Nazi gun policies were of no basic consequence: the democratic game had been lost long before, when legitimate authorities under the Weimar Republic would not or could not stop uniformed groups of Nazi terrorists from intimidating other citizens on the streets and in their meetings and when the courts and the Reich Ministry of Justice did not act firmly and consistently to punish the makers of any Nazi *Putsch* according to law. It is

Drawing by Liederman. ROTHCO.

not strong and firm governments but weak ones, incapable of exerting their regulatory and punitive powers, that are overthrown by tyrannies. Nonetheless, the American historical mythology about the protective value of guns has survived the modern technological era in all the glory of its naivete, and it has been taken over from the whites by some young blacks, notably the Panthers, whose accumulations of arms have thus far proved more lethal to themselves than to anyone else. In all societies the presence of small groups of uncontrolled and unauthorized men in unregulated possession of arms is recognized to be dangerous. A query therefore must ring in our heads: Why is it that in all other modern democratic societies those endangered ask to have such men disarmed, while in the United States alone they insist on arming themselves?

What Do You Think? _____

1. Some people have argued that guns are a symptom, not an effect, of violence. Would you agree? Why or why not?
2. How would you define gun control? Could a strict system of gun control be enforced? Why or why not?

---

7. Hijacking*

Hijacking of airliners has become relatively rare, yet airports continue to keep security tight. Is this still necessary?

A Delta Air Lines co-pilot, an airport security guard and a gunman were slain today in bursts of gunfire during an abortive attempt to hijack an Atlanta-bound Delta DC-9 jet as it was loading passengers at Baltimore-Washington International Airport.

Anne Arundel County police said the pilot and co-pilot were shot shortly after 7 a.m. by the would-be hijacker after he bolted from a line of passengers awaiting a security check and fatally shot an airport policeman at point-blank range.

Pronounced dead at 9:15 a.m. at the University of Maryland Hospital in Baltimore was the co-pilot, identified as Fred B. Jones of Dallas, Tex., who was shot in the head and chest. The pilot, Capt. Doug Lofton, was reported in critical condition at the hospital while undergoing surgery for gunshot wounds in the back and shoulders, with doctors quoted as saying, "The outlook is grave."

*Chris Lorenzo and William Basham.

The security guard was identified as George Ramsbury. The hijacking suspect was not identified. His body was taken to the Baltimore City Morgue, where fingerprints were taken and sent to the FBI.

A "box-like thing that smelled of gasoline" and was suspected of being a bomb was taken off the plane and placed on the runway several hundred feet away, police said.

A bomb blanket was used to cover the box, which resembled an attache case, and demolition experts later opened the container to find a crude bomb.

A stewardess aboard Delta Flight 523 was injured when she jumped from the plane as the shooting erupted, authorities said.

Thomas H. Farrow, an FBI spokesman, gave this account of the ordeal which lasted 10 minutes.

At 7:05 a.m., 41 passengers were boarding Flight 523 for Atlanta, which was scheduled to take off at 7:15. Eight passengers had already boarded.

Ramsbury, who has been on the airport police force for one year, was loading and screening passengers at the entrance of the ramp leading to the plane when a white male in his 40s came up behind him and shot him in the back of the head several times with a .22-caliber revolver.

Farrow said the suspected hijacker then ran down the ramp toward the plane. He was described as between 5 feet 6 and 5 feet 10, about 43 years old, of heavy build and wearing dark clothes.

Farrow said the man has not yet been identified and "we have no reason to believe that there are others involved at this time." His fingerprints are being checked.

The FAA spokesman said today that the last hijack attempt in the United States, coincidentally, was also at Baltimore-Washington Inter. on Jan 2, 1973.

The FAA said that during 1973, tighter security precautions at airports in this country turned up 57,651 weapons of all descriptions. The agency said that during the same period, 3,156 passengers were arrested and 3,439 others were denied boarding privileges.

What Do You Think? _____

1. Would you want airport security to remain very careful of passengers even though many are inconvenienced?
2. What effects have crime and violence had on our need for security?

8. Violence and the Comics

Who do you think wants violence? Does everyone enjoy violence on TV, in the movies, or in books?

What Do You Think? _____

1. What is the point of this comic strip?
2. Compare this strip with the one in Reading 5. How are they different? Similar? How would you explain these differences and similarities?

9. Violence and the Movies

Movies are changing. In what ways are the sorts of films described in this reading an effect of violence?

A. The Two Extremes*

There's no way to escape the fact that movies of violence are the choice of a large audience in the U.S. today. At the same time movie-goers write me that they are avoiding movies because they hate violence.

Understanding these two sections of the population is necessary for any one whose work involves movies. Seeking answers, I found one at the DeMille Theater on Broadway where a black audience (I was one of half a dozen white people in the theater) was seeing the first public screening of "Willie Dynamite," a movie about a black pimp.

On the opening day of a movie, reviews have not yet appeared in New York newspapers so the audience is there without much previous knowledge of the film, knowing only what the film's ads have told of the subject and stars.

As "Willie Dynamite" began the audience cheered the appearance of Roscoe Orman in the wild colors and styles of a pimp's contemporary wardrobe: red or purple custom-made suits, ankle-length coats and capes trimmed with white mink or ermine, headwear of equally imaginative materials and colors.

*   *   *   *   *

*Francis Taylor, "The Two Extremes," *Long Island Press,* February 3, 1974.

As the story unfolded the entire audience cheered each time Willie, the Number Two pimp who aims to make it to Number One, won a small victory. How he won, the value of his victory over terrorized girls, his glib rejection of other pimps' proposals to join forces . . . nothing mattered to the audience but Willie's winning.

His strutting alongside his luxurious car, with its fur-upholstered interior, his donning of still another fur coat, all these proved to the audience that violence was fine. Violence gave Willie power.

At one point, an elegant young man, dressed like Willie and accompanied by two young women dressed like Willie's stable of girls, leaned over to tap me on the shoulder.

"You ain't never seen nothing like that," he said to me. "White lady, you ain't seen no one like Willie."

"He was style," I answered.

"Yeah, but what he got is power," the man replied. "He got the money, that's power."

The black audience is usually a young audience and most of the young black population is part of the most powerless segment of our nation. Their parents had even less power. Their future promises little in the way of a share of social power.

The vicarious experience of power is what this audience gains from the violence and lawlessness of a movie like "Willie Dynamite."

White audiences are flocking to see "Magnum Force," starring Clint Eastwood, hero of many Italian-made Westerns that featured violence, virtue and bloodshed. But in those movies, which made Eastwood one of the world's top movie attractions, good men won in the end.

In "Magnum Force" Eastwood is Dirty Harry again, a police officer who makes his own laws and disposes of criminals as he sees fit. Harry has no need for courts, judges or ethics. His gun is his law. He has a personal code and he lives, while others die, by that code.

"Magnum Force" offers a conflict between Harry's code, directed against criminals, and a new code operating within the police department where four young veterans also take the law in their own hands. They decide a mobster should die, so they attack his home, killing him and every one who happens to be with him at a birthday party beside a swimming pool. Harry finds this too much of a good thing and thinks it's his job to find the mass killer.

Such a conflict offers the thrill of many bloody bodies, a chase, lots of suspense and shooting. Again the shared thrill of power seems to be operating.

* * * * *

The spread of this screened violence may offer a kind of safety valve today when many people feel that the nation is being run for the benefit of a very few individuals. But violence is not an answer to social ills and it cannot provide power to the powerless. Momentary victory is a final scene in many movies. What comes after that is not part of the script, but it is part of life.

Other audiences declare, with readers who wrote recently, that they'll   **73** stay home if their only movie fare is full of violence. Yet when they seek guidance from the rating code, they often find a movie full of violence has not been rated unsuitable for children. The ratings apparently find only sex obscene.

B. A Director Comments*

Barbara: Mr. Peckinpah has said, "I want to rub their noses in the violence of it all," and his films show blood spurting, sometimes violence in slow motion, and the works. . . . He is also a rather complicated man; he is a man who deals in violence and who brings the television hostesses roses, which makes it rather hard to talk too straight and seriously. And he wears dark glasses so we can't see what he looks like.

(A scene from "Alfredo Garcia" is run on the screen.)

Barbara: Why do you think it's good, entertaining, anything, to have this kind of gory, excessive violence?

Sam: I don't think it's excessive at all, Barbara. I really think we show violence as it is, and people will recognize it as it is. I don't put violence on the screen so that people can enjoy it. I want them to understand what it is . . . but unfortunately most people come to see it because they dig it, which is a study of human nature, and which makes me a little sick. . . .

Barbara: It can be said, or you have said, that the myth of the noble savage is bull, that law and order and grace and understanding are things that have to be taught, but then you *could* teach it. . . . That's in your power.

Sam: It's not in my power. I go where I'm kicked. I work for a living. . . .

Barbara: So what you are doing, in a sense, what you think you're doing, is to give people what they want.

Sam: No, I try to give them truth.

Barbara: And if the truth is gory and excessively violent . . . and excessively bloody.

Sam: Well, let's take Lieutenant Calley, for example, and he was convicted by the army of shooting a two-and-a-half-year-old child in the back, and President Nixon has just reduced his sentence so that he's now going to be coming out. . . . Let's talk about violence. . . .

What Do You Think? _____

1. Is TV or film or literature violence bad for people? Adults? Youth? Little children? Why or why not?

2. Should people be prevented from seeing violent films? Who should decide?

---

*Excerpt from interview of Sam Peckinpah by Barbara Walters on the "Today" show, reprinted by permission of National Broadcasting Company, Inc.

10. Personal Destruction*

The effects of violence on the life of a professional boxer.

TO A FIGHTER KILLED IN THE RING

In a gym in Spanish Harlem
boys with the eyes of starved leopards
flick jabs at your ghost
chained to a sandbag.

They smell in the air the brief truth of poverty
just as you once did:
                    "The weak don't get rich."

                    *   *   *   *   *

You made good.
Probably you were a bastard,
dreaming of running men down in a Cadillac
and tearing blouses off women.

And maybe in your dreams great black teeth
ran after you down dead-end alleyways
and the walls of your room
seemed about to collapse,
bringing with them a sky of garbage
and your father's leather strap.
And you sat up afraid you were dying
just as you had so many nights as a child.

                    *   *   *   *   *

Small bruises to the brain.
An accumulation
of years of being hit.

I will not forget that picture of you
hanging over the ropes, eyes closed,
completely wiped out.
Like a voice
lost in the racket of a subway train
roaring on under the tenements of Harlem.

---

11. Black Rage*

Two black psychiatrists illustrate, in part, the psychological impact of the American way of life on black people. What are these psychological effects?

Granting the limitations of stereotypes, we should nevertheless like to sketch a paradigmatic[1] black man. His characteristics seem so connected to employment that we call it "the postal-clerk syndrome." This man is always described as "nice" by white people. In whatever integrated setting he works, he is the standard against whom other blacks are measured. "If they were all only like him, everything would be so much better." He is passive, nonassertive, and nonaggressive. He has made a virtue of identification with the aggressor, and he has adopted an ingratiating and compliant manner. In public his thoughts and feelings are consciously shaped in the direction he thinks white people want them to be. The pattern begins in childhood when the mother may actually say: "You must be this way because this is the only way you will get along with Mr. Charlie."

This man renounces gratifications that are available to others. He assumes a deferential mask. He is always submissive. He must figure out "the man" but keep "the man" from deciphering him. He is prevalent in the middle and upper-middle classes, but is found throughout the social structure. The more closely allied to the white man, the more complete the picture becomes. He is a direct lineal descendant of the "house nigger" who was designed to identify totally with the white master. The danger he poses to himself and others is great, but only the surface of passivity and compliance is visible. The storm below is hidden.

A leading Negro citizen came to a therapy session with his wife, who was suffering from a severe and intractable melancholia. She had several times seriously attempted suicide. The last attempt was particularly serious. She was angry with her husband and berated him for never opening up and exposing his feelings.

*Excerpted from William H. Grier and Price M. Cobbs, *Black Rage*. Copyright © 1968 by William H. Grier and Price M. Cobbs, Basic Books, Inc., Publishers, New York.

[1]Exemplary.

For his part, the husband remained "nice." He never raised his voice above a murmur. His wife could goad him, but he was the epitome of understanding. He was amenable to all suggestions. His manner and gestures were deliberate, studied, and noninflammatory. Everything was understated. During the course of treatment he was involved in several civil rights crises. His public life was an extension of his private one, and he used such words as "moderation" and "responsibility." His entire life was a study in passivity, in how to play at being a man without really being one.

It would be easy to write off this man as an isolated passive individual, but his whole community looks upon his career as a success story. He made it in the system to a position of influence and means. And it took an aggressive, driving, determined man to make it against the odds he faced. We must ask how much energy is required for him to conceal his drive so thoroughly. And we wonder what would happen if his controls ever failed.

Starting with slavery, black people, and more particularly black men, have had to devise ways of expressing themselves uniquely and individually and in a manner that was not threatening to the white man. Some methods of giving voice to aggressive masculinity have become institutionalized. The most stylized is the posture of "playing it cool."

The playing-it-cool style repeats itself over and over again in all aspects of black life. It is an important means of expression and is widely copied in the larger white culture. A man may be overwhelmed with conflict, threatened with an eruption of feelings, and barely maintaining his composure, but he will present a serene exterior. He may fear the eruption of repressed feelings if they bring a loss of control, but an important aspect of his containment is the fear that his aggression will be directed against the white world and still bring swift punishment. The intrapsychic dynamics may be similar in a white man, but for the black man it is socially far more important that the facade be maintained.

Patients have come for treatment who have had one or two visits with a variety of psychiatrists, psychologists, and social workers. In many cases they were written off as having no significant pathology or as being "poor patients." The importance of the cool style is apparent when one realizes the cost and suffering required to maintain it. Those who practice it have raised to a high art a life style which seems a peculiarly black contribution to adaptation in this society. . . .

When all the repressive forces fail and aggression erupts, it is vital that we ask the right questions. The issue is not what caused the riots of the past few years—that is clear to any man who has eyes. Rather, we must ask: What held this aggression in check for so long and what is the nature of this breached barrier? Dare anyone try to reconstruct it?

The goods of America, piled high in the neighborhood stores, had been offered to them with a price tag that made work slavery and made balancing a budget a farce. The pressure was ever on parents to buy a television set, to buy kitchen appliances and new cars. The available jobs paid so poorly and the prices (plus interest) of goods were so high that if one made a purchase he was entering upon years of indebtedness.

The carrot held in front of the ghetto laborer is the consumer item—the auto, the TV, and the hi-fi set. If the poor black man falls into place in America, he takes whatever job is offered, receives minimal pay, purchases hard goods at harder prices, and teeters from insolvency to bankruptcy in the ghetto.

Exhausted, he was offered a stimulant in the form of the civil rights laws. When it became clear that they were nothing more than words from Washington, he kicked over the traces. He took a short cut. Instead of working for a lifetime to buy a piece of slum property which might fall at any moment and which he would likely never own anyway—instead of this treadmill, he burned it down. Instead of working for years to pay three times the usual cost of a television set, he broke a window and stole it. Instead of the desperate, frustrating search to find out which white man was friendly and which was hostile, he simply labeled them all the enemy. There never seemed to be a great deal of difference between friends and enemies anyway. So in a spontaneous blast he burned up the ghetto. And the wrong question continued to be asked: Why a riot in Detroit, where conditions were so good?

The worst slum and the best slum are very close together compared with the distance separating the world of black men and the world of whites. At bottom, America remains a slave country which happens to have removed the slave laws from the books. The question we must ask is: What held the slave rebellion in check for so long?

The racist tradition is pervasive and envelops every American. For black men it constitutes a heavy psychological burden. From the unemployed, illiterate ghetto dweller to the urbanized man living in an integrated setting, careful examination shows psychological scars. Black men fight one another, do violence to property, do hurtful things to themselves while nursing growing hatred for the system which oppresses and humiliates them. Their manhood is tested daily. As one patient expressed it: "The black man in this country fights the main event in Madison Square Garden every day."

What Do You Think?

1. According to these authors, how has the "system" affected black people? Why?
2. How might a black leader reply to the author's analysis? A white leader?

ACTIVITIES FOR INVOLVEMENT

1. Discuss with your classmates how you would react if
   a. Robberies in your neighborhood were constantly increasing;
   b. Murders within families were increasing;
   c. Revolutionaries in your area were bombing government buildings;

    d.   Factories and public works were pouring vast amounts of pollution into the air and water;

    e.   Different races or ethnic groups openly fought with each other;

    f.   Prisoners in the local jail frequently committed suicide.

2.   Develop a list of reactions to each of the situations in Activity 1, noting what you might do about each situation if you were (a) a private citizen, (b) a law enforcement officer, (c) a political leader, (d) a businessman, (e) a minority parent. Which situation would cause you to react most strongly? Least strongly?

3.   Interview a police officer, a political leader, a minority group member, and an office or factory worker about the effects of violence on them. Make up a set of interview questions that will reveal their reactions to violence. For example, you might find out if more police protection has been demanded; if locks and bolts have been purchased for cars and homes; if guns or other weapons have been purchased; or if insurance has been taken out or increased on life and property. At the end of the polling, compare the responses offered by each of these groups. How would you explain any similarities or differences that appear?

4.   Some people say that the chief effect of violence is more violence. Find out if this seems to be true or not by doing research on several historical events. Collect information on the Detroit riots of 1967, the Memorial Day Massacre of 1937, the Chicago Convention of 1968, and the Hatfield-McCoy feud of 1873–1888. In each case, did the violence subside or continue? If it did continue, can we be *sure* that the event *caused* more violence? Explain.

5.   Examine one or more works of literature (such as Richard Wright's *Black Boy,* Norman Mailer's *The Naked and the Dead,* or Mario Puzo's *The Godfather*) that include experiences with violence. Study the main characters in each book and report on their reactions to violence. In what ways, if any, are they similar to any of the reactions in this chapter? Different?

6.   Richard Rubenstein, in his book *Rebels in Eden,* contends that violence —political violence, in particular—works to produce social change. He feels that social change is usually for the good of the society as a whole, and that violence pushes change forward. Test his idea by considering whether or not violence has, in fact, worked to better social conditions in the following instances:

- Have prison riots resulted in prison reform and better conditions for the inmates?

- Have ghetto riots resulted in better conditions for the area?

- Have organized protests by the poor brought them better housing? More jobs? Higher welfare payments?

- Have civil rights marches resulted in more equality for blacks? Chicanos? Indians?

- Have bombings of Russian government buildings in the United States bettered the position of Jews in Russia?
- Have sometimes violent labor strikes brought better working conditions? Higher wages?

Select one or more of these questions and try to collect examples that you believe support or refute them. Compare your examples with those in Rubenstein's book. Perhaps you can make up your own question to answer. In general, does the evidence agree with, or oppose, the idea that violence brings social change?

7. This chapter has suggested a number of possible effects of violence. Possible effects include:

- More violence
- Fear
- Corruption in government
- Less respect for the rights of other people
- Riots
- Increased sales of guns and other weapons
- Apathy
- Increased demand for "law and order"
- Greater respect for police officers
- Financial loss
- Increased anxiety and worry over personal safety
- Glorification of violent acts and violent people
- Psychological breakdown

Rank these effects in order from most to least violent and then explain your rankings. What other effects, if any, would you add to the list?

6
HOW CAN
WE DEAL
WITH VIOLENCE?

What are some alternatives to violence? Some people think this question should not even be asked, for they view violence as a necessary part of social life. Violence, after all, is one way of solving disputes and of controlling the destinies of other people.

Many people who think along these lines, however, though they support the use of violence to attain certain goals, fear its use in the wrong hands. Too much violence may undermine and even destroy a society. Hence the search for alternatives to violence becomes a necessity.

We have examined several different forms of violence in the preceding chapters: political, economic, psychological, criminal, rational and irrational. The following readings suggest a few ways by which some of the problems posed by violence may be approached and perhaps lessened.

1. Condition People Against Killing*

Might it be possible to create a taboo against killing? That is what the author of this reading suggests.

What if, in the past, the human race had conditioned its children against killing as rigorously as it conditioned them against sex? Until this modern age, the sex inhibition was fairly successful in keeping youngsters out of trouble, whatever other damage it happened to do.

A social prohibition against killing would not do any other damage, and might have inhibited people from slaughtering one another through the generations. "Aggressiveness," of course, will never be bred out of humans, but aggressiveness can stop quite short of killing.

The main reason this has not been done—even though homicidal violence can be shown to be a far greater threat to our species than sexual permissiveness—is that the state has always needed its warriors. If men will not kill, but will instead peacefully try to adjust their differences by reason or by other contests of skill and strength, then the leaders have lost their prime power over the masses.

The Commandment "Thou shalt not kill!" has been interpreted in all Western countries to tailor Christianity to national goals, rather than to fit the country to the religious model. Private citizens are not allowed to kill for private reasons; but as public soldiers, they are encouraged to kill for "civic" reasons that are often just as evil.

It is extraordinary that copulation, which is a life-giving and joyous activity, has been so hedged with restrictions, inhibitions and taboos; while killing, which goes against all divine, human and rational principles, has

*Excerpted from Sidney J. Harris, "Let's Concentrate Taboos on Killing," Publishers-Hall Syndicate, March 26, 1971.

always been rewarded with honors, rank, medals and supreme power by the state.

The strength of "incest taboos" over the centuries, for instance, indicates how strongly the past can imprint repressions upon the young if it sincerely believes them and carries them out effectively. A similar "killing taboo" · against members of our own species could be equally exercised, were it not that the ruling caste of every social order is unwilling to do this for fear of losing its ultimate authority of force.

The state kills "enemies"; it kills "traitors"; it kills "revolutionaries"; it kills "criminals"; it even kills mere "undesirables." And it is rarely the populace themselves who decide who such enemies and traitors and revolutionaries and criminals and undesirables are; it is their leaders, who wish to preserve themselves in power by all means.

If we were really serious about it, our children could be so conditioned from birth that taking another person's life would be an unimaginable horror that only the most demented or perverted could commit. Instead, we breed a race of moral idiots who think it is glorious to do for the state what it is forbidden to do singly.

What Do You Think? _____

1. Would you agree with the author's notion as to why violence has never been banned from society? Why or why not?
2. How realistic is the author's proposal? Who might oppose it? Who might favor it? Why?

2. Give Treatment to the Violence-Prone*

Next, an argument that violent people should be helped, and helped quickly. Is violence a form of mental illness?

The potentially violent person can be treated effectively with a variety of methods: tranquilizers, individual and group psychotherapy, conditioning techniques including hypnosis, and psychodrama. Chances for a successful outcome are equal to, or better than, those of the average schizophrenic.[1] The treatment would, though, be more efficacious[2] if it were given in a hospital

*From *Violence: Causes and Solutions,* edited by Dr. Renatus Hartogs and Eric Artzt. Copyright © 1970 by Renatus Hortogs and Eric Artzt. Reprinted by permission of the publisher, Dell Publishing Co., Inc.
[1]Person suffering from a psychosis characterized by delusions and hallucinations.
[2]Effective.

setting rather than on an outpatient basis. Maintaining a violence-prone individual outside while he undergoes treatment, as now is often true, naturally incurs greater risk. . . .

Treatment of the potentially violent in a mental hospital is the preferred way of therapeutic approach; it serves to impress the patient with the seriousness of his disorder. In addition to the evaluative procedures discussed above, it should consist in drug therapy, with alternate sessions of individual interviews, to impart a feeling of social ease.

Treatment of the violence-prone in a rehabilitation center should focus on his wish to acquire a definite, socially acceptable identity. This type of patient profits a great deal from learning and working together with others; he has to be given the opportunity to form proper identifications and alliances. He must also be given the chance to dissociate from other, similarly violent individuals, since violence is highly contagious. In group therapy, though, several violence-prone patients can be treated simultaneously, providing considerable benefit to all of them. Regular medication can be helpful, but the dose may be small.

The individual should be led to analyze and resolve problems. Work therapy can help accomplish this. The emphasis is on creativity, no matter how primitive or naive it is, permitting the violence to be expressed in a sublimated way.

With successful treatment, the potentially violent person learns to appreciate the necessity—even the joy—of exercising reliable inner control, while additionally satisfying his need for identity and prestige. Treating violence is, of course, going about it the hard way. With few exceptions, individuals can be prevented from ever becoming violence-prone. The techniques that parents can use are different from some discussed so far, but the concepts behind them are similar.

The child must first of all be taught that reward is not likely to come without effort and planning; it is not immediately granted, and it may fail to meet expectations. But life is filled with such disappointments. The child should realize that the mastery of these frustrations without temper tantrums is a major part of what it is to be grown up.

At the same time, other areas of challenge and mastery should be opened to him, in the intellectual, emotional, social, and physical realms. With achievement comes self-confidence, and this provides a sound basis for the development of self-control.

What Do You Think?

1. Are people who engage in violence mentally sick? All kinds of violence? Explain.

2. Can violence-prone individuals be forced to undergo psychiatric help? Should they be?

3. Would the proper training of children to face disappointments realistically, plus offering them the opportunity for achievement, help to reduce violence? Why or why not?

3. Offer Physical Substitutes*

Next, a suggestion that we face frankly and realistically the fact that men, especially the young, need outlets for their energy, that they need to work off their aggressive instincts in some way. The author suggests some means by which this might be accomplished. Might his ideas work?

[Violence] may well continue on a rising scale, until we can discover what James[1] called a "moral equivalent for war." He thought he had found it. He wanted to draft "the whole youthful population" into a peacetime army to serve in "the immemorial human warfare against nature." What he had in mind was a sort of gigantic Civilian Conservation Corps, in which every youngster would spend a few years at hard and dangerous labor—consigned to "coal and iron mines, to freight trains, to fishing fleets in December . . . to road-building and tunnel-making." When he wrote, a half century ago, this idea sounded plausible, because the need for such work seemed limitless.

Today, however, his prescription is harder to apply. In many parts of the globe, the war against nature has ended, with nature's unconditional surrender. Automation, moreover, has eliminated most dangerous and physically demanding jobs; our mines and freight trains are over-manned, our roads are now built with earth-moving machines rather than pick and shovel.

Nevertheless, so far as I can see, James's idea is still our best starting point. And already an encouraging number of people are groping for ways to make it work, in the different and more difficult circumstances of our time.

A few have found personal, unofficial answers. The young people who join the civil-rights movement in the South, for example, are encountering hardship, violence, and occasionally death in a cause that is obviously genuine; they aren't playing games. But the movement can accommodate only a limited number of volunteers, and presumably it will go out of business eventually. . . . In the North, civil-rights work has often turned out to be less satisfying, emotionally, because The Enemy is harder to identify and the goals are less clear. As a result, its young partisans sometimes have drifted into a kind of generalized protest, carrying placards for almost anything . . . that is, they have ended up with another form of game playing.

President Kennedy, who understood thoroughly the youthful need for struggle and self-sacrifice, had the Jamesian principle in mind when he started the Peace Corps. It remains the most successful official experiment in this direction, and it led to the Job Corps and several experiments in the domestic Antipoverty Program. How they will work out is still an open question. At least they are a public recognition that the country has to do *something*. If we

---

*Excerpted from John Fischer, "Substitutes for Violence." Copyright © 1965 by Minneapolis Star and Tribune Co., Inc. Reprinted from the January 1966 issue of *Harper's Magazine* by permission of the author.
[1]William James (1842–1910), philosopher and psychologist.

Youths cleaning oil spill from beach at Galveston, Texas.

don't—if we continue to let millions of young men sit around, while the adrenalin bubbles and every muscle screams for action, with no outlet in sight but a desk job at best and an unemployment check at worst—then we are asking for bad trouble. Either we can find ways to give them action, in some useful fashion, or we can look forward to a rising surge of antisocial violence. In the latter case we may, a decade from now, remember the Fort Lauderdale beach riots as a mere boyish prank.

What I am suggesting, of course, is that all of us—especially our businessmen, sociologists, and political leaders—ought to invest a good deal more effort, ingenuity, and money in the search for acceptable substitutes for violence. How many industries have really tried to create interesting and physically demanding jobs for young people? Have the paper companies, for instance, figured out how many foresters they might use, if they were to develop their timber reserves for camping, hunting, and fishing, as well as for wood pulp? And are they sure such a venture would not be profitable?

To take care of the population explosion, we are going to have to duplicate all of our present college buildings within the next 20 years. Has any university looked into the possibility of using prospective students to do some of the building? Maybe every able-bodied boy should be required to labor on the campus for six months as a brick-layer or carpenter before he is admitted to classes?

Cleaning up our polluted rivers is a task worthy of Paul Bunyan, and one we can't postpone much longer. What governor has thought of mobilizing a state Youth Corps to do part of the job? How many husky youngsters might be deployed, axes in hand, to chop down billboards along our highways and replace them with trees?

Why, my wife asks me, is all that necessary? Wouldn't it be simpler for you men to stop acting like savages? Since you realize that belligerence is no longer a social useful trait, why don't you try to cultivate your gentler and more humane instincts? Are you saying that You Can't Change Human Nature?

No, that isn't quite what I'm saying. I recognize that human nature changes all the time. Cannibalism, for example, is now fairly rare, and polygamy (at least in its more open form) has been abandoned by a number of cultures. Some day (I hope and believe) the craving for violence will leach out of the human system. But the reversal of an evolutionary process takes a long time. For a good many generations, then, the old Adam is likely to linger in our genes; and during that transitional period, probably the best we can hope for is to keep him reasonably quiet with some variant of William James's prescription.

What Do You Think? _____

1. Who might oppose the author's suggestions? How might their opposition be countered? What is your position?

2. Would the author of the first reading in this chapter support the author's ideas? Why or why not?

4. Enact Gun Controls*

Former Police Commissioner Murphy of New York argues that the hand gun is at the core of violence in the United States. He argues for the control of weapons. Is this a realistic alternative?

What wife would place a $50,000 value on her husband's life? What child would regard any amount of money as a substitute for his father? These questions need no answer for no person can place a price tag on the life of a loved one.

Recently after a widely publicized White House conference summoned to discuss ways of coping with the wave of police shootings, the single suggestion advanced by the federal officials who presided was a proposal for federal

*Excerpted from Patrick V. Murphy, "Are Gun Controls Necessary?" *Long Island Press,* August 8, 1971.

legislation authorizing a $50,000 payment to the family of any policemen slain in the line of duty.

As with insurance from any quarter, cash payments on death do cushion the financial shock caused by the loss of the head of the household, but no one proposes insurance as a substitute for prudent protection designed to save lives.

The causes of violence in our society, including violence directed at police officers, are indeed complex; and tragic slayings of policemen will not be eliminated as long as crime, tension, and bitterness survive. But there is one step that can be taken immediately to reduce the level of violence and the number of lethal confrontations, both with policemen and with other law-abiding citizens.

More stringent controls ordained by the federal government over the manufacture, distribution and sale of handguns and parts for handguns are virtually necessary if there is to be a serious and sincere effort to protect the lives of citizens, including policemen, who deserve protection from murderous attacks. . . .

How many more widows must bury their husbands, policemen and private citizens alike, before it is clear whether disarming criminals and potential criminals serves the "best purposes" of this country? We simply cannot wait and watch any longer as our people are slaughtered simply because guns are within reach when tempers flare, or during the commission of a crime. . . .

Opting for a cash payment to the survivors of slain policemen while deferring or rejecting more stingent controls over deadly weapons is like opposing moves for increased auto safety because most drivers carry insurance that will provide some money to the victim of an automobile crash.

Make no mistake about it. The handgun is at the core of violence in inclining people toward a deadly response to a situation and providing the means for drastic action.

Over 200,000 gun crimes are committed in this country each year. The Eisenhower Commission found that two-thirds of all homicides, one-third of all robberies and one-fifth of all aggravated assaults are committed with a firearm—usually a handgun. Nearly 3,000 Americans die every year from firearm accidents alone. . . .

What we need is the urgent concern of both legislative and executive branches of the federal government to provide us with the tools that will enable the police to choke off the sources of the basic instruments of violence in our society. This is a program for direct action designed to protect our police officers and the communities they serve.

What Do You Think?_____

2. Do most people really abhor violence? If so, why are gun controls not put into effect?

1. How practical are Chief Murphy's ideas? How would they compare to Hofstadter's ideas in Reading 6, Chapter 5? Explain.

5. "If Guns Were Outlawed, Only Outlaws Would Have Guns"*

The above heading appears frequently as a bumper sticker and expresses the position of the National Rifle Association. The NRA holds that denying people the right to own guns for their own self-defense is an encouragement, not a deterrent, of crime. Would an armed citizenry prevent violence?

The NRA firmly rejects the premise that firearms are a major factor in a rise in crime. Is it the inanimate tool that is responsible for crime or is it persons with distorted, twisted minds? Consider the deaths of the fifty-seven police officers killed in a recent year. We can even look back further than that, and we find that three-fourths of the murderers of police officers for the past five years have had prior records of arrest; one half had prior records of grave assault-type crimes; one-third were on parole or probation when they committed the murder! J. Edgar Hoover, [former] Director of the Federal Bureau of Investigation, [once] stated: "Of the fourteen Special Agents killed in gun battles, twelve were slain by criminals who had been previously selected for parole or other types of leniency."

The police strength throughout our country is less than two police employees per 1,000 people. Such a figure is possible only because 99 per cent of our people are law-abiding. After a recent Supreme Court decision favoring criminals, the police chief of one of our large cities commented: "If our hands are tied further, citizens will have greater need than ever for armed self-protection."

Certainly law-abiding, God-fearing men and women have a right to protect their loved ones, their homes, and their places of business against the criminal element of our society. And it is this criminal element at which our legislative guns should be aimed, not a scatter-gun shot at every citizen. Self-protection is one of the basic laws of nature. A law-abiding man with a gun is not to be feared by society or by the government. If the government fears the people, then it follows that the people will begin to fear their government.

Everyone knows that the millions of fine citizens who own guns are not a lunatic fringe or trigger-happy morons as suggested by a few writers inclined to muckraking and sensational journalism. And likewise everyone knows that, although disarming the American citizen is a primary goal spelled out in the captured Communist document "Rules for Bringing About a Revolution," proponents of restrictive firearms policies are not necessarily communists, pacifists, professional do-gooders, or publicity-seekers.

---

*Excerpted from James B. Trefethen, *Americans and Their Guns,* Stackpole Company, Harrisburg, Pa,; 1967. Copyright © 1967, The National Rifle Association of America.

"Firearms have been a far greater force in keeping the law than breaking it." Compare this statement by the NRA with the premise of Reading 4. With which position do you agree? What evidence can you offer to support or refute either statement?

---

6. Practice Nonviolence*

Protest marches and demonstrations are one way of achieving recognition and of influencing social attitudes. Mahatma Gandhi of India thought that social-protest movements should be free of violence. He influenced others to think in the same way, thus giving rise to the theory and practice of nonviolence. An American example of rules for nonviolent demonstrations is given here. Can nonviolence be an effective alternative to violence?

Discipline for Public Witness Demonstrations

Achievement of these objectives is greatly enhanced if all demonstrators conduct themselves in a friendly and orderly manner. A disorderly demonstration is more likely to arouse opposition than support. Violence on the part of the demonstrators will almost certainly retard, rather than advance, the work of the peace movement. Demonstrations can be an opportunity to communicate our friendliness and concern for others in and outside of the demonstration and to begin to express specifically the concept of altruistic love. The following discipline is designed to facilitate this expression.

All persons are asked to accept the following discipline during the time they are participating in this demonstration. If you feel you cannot cooperate with all of the aspects of the discipline, *please leave the demonstration at an appropriate time.* The sponsors have no desire to limit spontaneity or dictate to the consciences of others. The discipline exists only to minimize the likelihood of rioting and violence and to increase the power of the demonstrations.

1. We will not use physical violence regardless of what may be done to us by others.
2. Our attitude toward persons who may oppose us will be one of understanding, and of respect for the right of others to hold and express whatever views they wish.
3. We will not be violent in our attitude, make hostile remarks, shout or call

---

*Excerpted from Arthur & Lila Weinberg (eds.), "Peace Organizations Give Their Rules for Public Witness Demonstrations," *Instead of Violence,* Boston: Beacon Press, 1965.

names. If singing or chanting is indicated, it will be in a manner consistent with the nonviolent spirit of the demonstration.

4. We will adhere to the planned program of action for each demonstration, unless a change of plan is communicated to us by the demonstration's sponsors or their representatives. We will not initiate any unannounced action, unless it has been explicitly approved by the sponsors.

5. We recognize that conducting an orderly demonstration depends upon mutual cooperation and respect between participants and those who have organized and are responsible for the demonstration. (If requests are made for action which you feel are unwise, you will have an opportunity to discuss your complaint fully with the responsible persons after the demonstration, if it is not possible at the time. If a request is made which you cannot accept, please quietly disassociate yourself from the demonstration.)

6. If questioned by passers-by, representatives of the press or other mass media, participants are encouraged to express their own opinion about themselves, their reasons for joining the demonstration, etc., making clear that these are their personal convictions. However, where possible, all questions concerning the policies of the demonstration should be referred to the sponsors or their representatives. The questioner should be given a copy of the demonstration's official leaflet.

7. In our contact with the police and other officials, we will:
   A. Maintain an attitude of understanding for the responsibilities with which they are charged.
   B. Be courteous at all times.
   C. Be completely open in announcing what we plan to do.
   D. Accept all requests which are reasonable.

8. We will be as truthful as possible in all statements.

9. *In case of violence.* Demonstration plans will always be announced to the police and in general their cooperation should be expected. However, in a large crowd there is always the possibility of violence from arbitrary police interference, passers-by or participants. In such situations, the demonstrators must carefully follow the directions of the sponsors and their representatives.

The demonstrators might be requested to disperse as quickly and as quietly as possible in order to avoid incidents. It is usually better to take up grievances with the authorities after the demonstration than to try to settle them on the spot.

Sitting down might, in some cases, reduce the number of possible injuries in an emergency situation. Since sitting will probably be interpreted as civil disobedience and noncompliance, such action should be undertaken only upon the specific requests of the demonstration's sponsors or their representatives,[1]

[1]Demonstrators who have sat down and are offering nonviolent resistance to the police are urged to act in a way that does not imply disrespect for the police but is designed to prevent injuries and show peaceful intent.

or if it is agreed upon in advance as the method of action of the particular demonstration.

Those who witness molestation or brutality on the part of the police may render a service by making a note of the numbers on the badges of those involved.

What Do You Think?

1. What instances can you find where the use of nonviolent techniques were effective? Ineffective? Why?
2. Would these rules lessen or increase the chance of violence? Why?

7. Free Speech*

The next selection was written in 1920 by a noted rabbi. The author argues against violence of any kind—governmental, group or personal and offers what he believes to be a major alternative to violence. Would you agree?

I abhor bloodshed. I believe that human life and the human personality are sacred, and that human life may not be taken at any time. I do not believe in war between one people and another, and I did not believe in this past war, and I do not believe in the next. I recount these personal items because, as a pacifist, I may differ greatly from this or that radical group. I stand nevertheless for the right of every man and every group to advocate any and every governmental, political, economic, spiritual change, no matter what be the doctrines they preach and no matter what be the methods they talk and write about. I am as much opposed to the use of machine guns and bombs and hand grenades and poison gas by the workers, by the proletariat, as to the use of these instruments of hatred and murder by organized governments. But I believe that every man and every political and economic organization have the right to formulate their doctrines in speech and in writing freely. Only when speech and writing are left in the background and actual overt acts of physical violence and bloodshed are committed has a people's government the right to intervene. Under all circumstances we must maintain the right of free speech, without qualification and without let or hindrance.

Government has no right to interfere with ideas, with programs, with opinions formulated in speech or in writing, no matter what these ideas and opinions may be. If men wish to advocate the use of force and violence in the change and overthrow of government, let them advocate it openly, above

*Excerpted from Judah Magnes, "Judah Magnes Supports the Right of All Men to Speak Freely," in Arthur and Lila Weinberg (eds.), *Instead of Violence,* Boston: Beacon Press, 1965.

ground, frankly. Then let you and me meet them by reason if we can, by argument, by free discussion. Prove them wrong, if we can, by trying to remove the underlying causes of their impatience and their skepticism. It is injustice, cruelty, terrorization of the weak by the strong, spiritual and physical slavery which they wish to force out of existence. Can we show by precept and by example that these age-long iniquities[1] can be removed from the lives of men in other ways than through force and violence? If even then men wish to take upon themselves the burden and the odium of writing or talking in advocacy of force and violence, let them. It is old American doctrine that freedom of discussion, the conflict of ideas, debate, argument, will bring out the true and will suppress the false. It is old American faith that the masses of the people are sound at heart and in mind, and that it is possible to reason with them, to convince them through information, through candor, through mental integrity. It is an old American idea that government is based upon free consent, and that it is perpetuated or changed through an informed and honest public opinion.

What Do You Think? _____

Some people are opposed to the author's suggestion that government has no right to interfere with ideas no matter what these ideas may be. Who might be so opposed? Why? Can you think of an idea that should *not* be expressed? Ever? On what basis?

_____

8. Rehabilitate Criminals*

Having pointed out the problems of prisons, former Attorney General Ramsey Clark offers solutions to aid the prisoners and to give them useful roles in society. He feels that prisons cause more violence than they prevent, and offers a complete plan to lessen crime and diminish violence. Would his suggestions reduce violence?

The goal of modern correction must be not revenge, not penance, not punishment, but rehabilitation. The theory of rehabilitation is based on the belief that healthy, rational people will not injure others. Rehabilitated, an individual will not have the capacity—will not be able to bring himself—to injure another nor to take or destroy property. Rehabilitation is individual salvation. What achievement can give society greater satisfaction than to afford the offender the chance, once lost, to live at peace, to fulfill himself and to help

[1]Gross injustices.
*Excerpted from Ramsey Clark, "When Punishment Is a Crime," *Playboy,* November 1970. Copyright © 1970 by Ramsey Clark. Reprinted by permission of Simon and Schuster.   **93**

others? Rehabilitation is also the one clear way that the criminal justice system can significantly reduce crime. We know who the most frequent offenders are; there is no surprise when they strike again. Even if nothing but selfish interest impelled us, rehabilitation would be worth the effort. When it works, it reduces crime, reduces the cost of handling prisoners, reduces the cost of the criminal justice system and even relieves pressure to provide the basic and massive reforms that are necessary to affect the underlying causes of crime.

From the moment a person is charged with crime, correction personnel should work toward the day he will return to unrestrained community life. Accused persons should be released pending trial. They may need help and can be given it, including supervision that protects the public and that is not inconsistent with their presumed innocence. Many of the personal problems pushing a person toward crime are visible long before the first arrest. They were having trouble in school and dropped out or were unemployed, running with a gang, drinking too much, taking dope, or were obviously mentally unstable. Once the individual is arrested, these problems should immediately be identified; counseling, guidance and treatment can then begin.

Following a conviction, analysis of the individual's physical, mental, emotional, family and social condition must be made. The prisoner should be allowed to review this analysis, which will be the basis for the design of his individual program. It should be available to the judge and carefully analyzed before sentencing. . . .

If rehabilitation is the goal, only the indeterminate sentence should be used in all cases. Such a sentence sets an outer limit beyond which the state may no longer restrain the liberty of the individual. The prisoner may be unconditionally released or gradually released under restrictive conditions designed to assure rehabilitation at any time within the period of the sentence. Techniques of release may begin with the family visits of a few hours' duration. Later, a man may be able to take on part-time or full-time employment or attend school in a community correction center. Overnight visits with the family might follow and finally, the conditional release, requiring continued schooling with good performance, employment at a productive level or a stable family situation.

What motivation does a prisoner condemned to seven certain years have in the first, the second or even the fifth year? He is waiting. A program designed to rehabilitate him must wait also. There is no incentive. But even in the early months of the long indeterminate sentence—say for a maximum period of ten years—the prisoner can see the chance to work days, to attend school, to learn a trade, to visit home, to move to a community correction location. The light at the end of the tunnel is visible and it always looks good. It can be a goal —perhaps the first goal of a lifetime.

The day of the indeterminate sentence is coming, but slowly. The practice is less than 15 years old in the Federal system, but the number of indeterminate sentences given in the system doubled between 1964 and 1969 and today the sentence is used in more than 20 percent of all convictions to prison. Yet there remain entire Federal judicial districts where an indeterminate sentence has never been given, while some enlightened Federal judges give little else.

No correctional system in the country is yet staffed to make effective use of the indeterminate sentence, but this is hardly an argument against it. In any system where professional skills are available, they would be put to better use. Even in those systems with no skills, the change to indeterminate sentencing would at least give the prisoner the chance, however remote, of release at any time.

There are risks, of course, in the use of the indeterminate sentence, as there are in any technique. And it does not, obviously, guarantee rehabilitation. It is only the beginning—only an opportunity. Parole authorities and prison personnel can abuse this additional power, use it arbitrarily or fail to use it through timidity. But we must reform personnel standards and techniques in the system anyway, and any flagrant abuses could be expected to come under judicial review.

Meaningful vocational training in high-employment fields is the best program for many. Throughout the history of Federal correction, most prisoners have been faced with two choices—remaining in the total custody of a prison or being released to the community with insignificant parole supervision. While the Federal Prison Industries program trained and meaningfully employed some, their projects took place within the prison environment and the skills learned were minimal and often in trades in which employment was hard to find. In the early days, it was agriculture, still a dominant occupation in some state prison systems. Later, textile work, bricklaying, tire recapping, auto repair and metalwork were offered some. Now automatic data processing and white-collar training are afforded a few.

In 1965, in what seemed a bold step, the Federal prison system first placed prisoners in normal community employment situations. A work-release program authorized by Congress permitted prisoners to leave in the morning for a place of employment, work there during the day and return to prison when the workday ended. Prisoners were cautiously selected and assigned to the program, nearly always during the last months of their incarceration. Other inmates often made it clear to those chosen that they had better not abuse the opportunity. Among the first jobs offered prisoners in the program were carpentry, auto repair and bookkeeping. One young man traveled 60 miles a day by commercial bus from the Federal institution at Seagoville, Texas, worked a half day in the dean's office at a state college, took three courses and made three A's.

The strain was great on these men, of course. The meaning of imprisonment had never been so clear. Some admitted the great difficulties in returning to prison at night. But by the end of 1968, thousands of men had been through the program and fewer than one in twenty had failed to comply with all the conditions. Alcohol was the cause of failure in nearly two thirds of the cases; the tavern simply looked too inviting after work and the prospect of returning to prison too dismal. We should hardly be surprised that five percent failed: **95**

Prisoner, shown in the woodshop of his home during a
weekend pass, attends college while serving a 30-year
sentence for murder.

With no program, 50 percent of all prisoners fail when finally released. As to
the five percent who sought to escape, all were caught and returned to prison,
where they served more time. People do not really escape from prison success-
fully. In the history of the Federal Bureau of Prisons, hundreds of thousands
have been imprisoned and thousands have escaped, but fewer than 20 have not
been recaptured or otherwise accounted for. . . .

Work release, halfway houses, pre-release guidance centers—these are
only the beginnings. Community supervision is the future of correction. Whenever competent authorities decide that prisoners have reached a reasonable
level of rehabilitation, they should be moved from conventional prisons to such
community facilities as a floor of a Y.M.C.A., a wing in an apartment building
or a house. In such settings, men can learn to live in an environment approach-

ing the kind to which they must adjust before being released. Their freedom, their associations, their schedule can be controlled, as necessary, to help achieve rehabilitation. Family visits can begin, followed by church attendance, if desired, perhaps a movie or a date and later a whole weekend. . . .

As soon as possible, schooling should be resumed for those capable of it. In Federal youth centers, some 90 percent of the inmates are high school and junior high school dropouts. Without special tutoring to get them somewhere near their appropriate grade level, their chances for a life free of crime are slight.

America is a nation with the skills and resources to provide the necessary elements of rehabilitation: Physical and mental health, all the education a youngster can absorb, vocational skills for the highest trade he can master, a calm and orderly environment away from anxiety and violence, life among people who care, who love—with these, a boy can begin again. With these, he can regain a reference for life, a sense of security and self-assurance amid all the pressures of modern community life. These attitudes will not be developed in a laboratory. They must be developed in the community itself—first, sometimes, in the prison community, but finally in the open society in which the individual must make his way by himself.

What Do You Think?_____

1.   Would you agree with the idea that prisons should rehabilitate? Why or why not?
2.   Is prison reform an alternative to violence? All violence? Explain.

---

9. Restructure the System*

William O. Douglas, then Associate Justice of the Supreme Court, points out that our society is offered a choice of where it will go, toward less or toward greater violence, and that to prevent the latter we must restructure many of our existing institutions. Would you agree?

. . . The risk of violence is a continuing one in our society, because the oncoming generation has two deep-seated convictions:

First. The Welfare program works in reverse by syphoning off billions of dollars to the rich and leaving millions of people hungry and other millions feeling the sting of discrimination.

*Excerpted from Points of Rebellion, by William O. Douglas. Copyright © 1969, 1970 by William O. Douglas. Reprinted by permission of Random House, Inc.

Second. The special interests that control government use its powers to favor themselves and to perpetuate regimes of oppression, exploitation, and discrimination against the many.

There are only two choices: A police state in which all dissent is suppressed or rigidly controlled; or a society where law is responsive to human needs.

If society is to be responsive to human needs, a vast restructuring of our laws is essential.

Realization of this need means adults must awaken to the urgency of the young people's unrest—in other words there must be created an adult unrest against the inequities and injustices in the present system. If the government is in jeopardy, it is not because we are unable to cope with revolutionary situations. Jeopardy means that either the leaders or the people do not realize they have all the tools required to make the revolution come true. The tools and the opportunity exist. Only the moral imagination is missing.

If the budget of the Pentagon were reduced from 80 billion dollars to 20 billion it would still be over twice as large as that of any other agency of government. Starting with vast reductions in its budget, we must make the Pentagon totally subordinate in our lives.

The poor and disadvantaged must have lawyers to represent them in the normal civil problems that now haunt them.

Laws must be revised so as to eliminate their present bias against the poor. Neighborhood credit unions would be vastly superior to the finance companies with their record of anguished garnishments.

Hearings must be made available so that the important decisions of federal agencies may be exposed to public criticism before they are put into effect.

The food program must be drastically revised so that its primary purpose is to feed the hungry rather than to make the corporate farmer rich.

A public sector for employment must be created that extends to meaningful and valuable work. It must include many arts and crafts, the theatre, industries; training of psychiatric and social workers, and specialists in the whole gamut of human interest. . . .

The constitutional battle of the Blacks has been won, but equality of opportunity has, in practice, not yet been achieved. There are many, many steps still necessary. The secret is continuous progress.

Whatever the problem, those who see no escape are hopelessly embittered. A minimum necessity is measurable change.

What Do You Think? _____

1. Which of the author's suggestions do you think are most feasible? Least? Explain your reasoning.
2. How might Ramsey Clark (Reading 8) react to Justice Douglas's proposals? Freud? Others?

10. Act Like the Fox*

The Fox strikes again! When pollution or ecological destruction rears its ugly head, an unknown citizen of Chicago—the Fox—leaps into action. Taking the law into his (?) own hands, the Fox and cohorts attack the polluters, large and small, and pay them back in property damage. What do you think of the Fox's actions?

In the past few years there has been a ground swell of public resistance to needless contamination of our lakes and rivers. Save the Great Lakes! Some groups rely on court suits to stop polluters. Others picket or rally public opinion through newspaper advertisements. At least one man prefers direct action in the battle to stop pollution.

He signs himself "the Fox." With a small group of conspirators, he wages anonymous war against water polluters near Chicago—plugging pipes that pour chemicals into streams, depositing dead skunks at the homes of offenders. He has become a folk hero, and the bane of local police.

In Chicago I let it be known as widely as possible that I wanted to interview the Fox. Weeks later, at my home near Washington, D.C., I received a long-distance phone call from a mild-voiced man. "People call me the Fox. I hear you'd like to talk to me."

The next week I met the Fox and his two chief confederates. I still have no clue to the identity of the three men.

What does the Fox look like? I can tell you this: He does not resemble the flashing-eyed crusader I'd expected. His eyes twinkled when I asked why he'd begun his life of crime.

But his answer was serious. "I've never stopped being a law-abiding citizen. It's those companies I visit that are breaking the law—the moral law. They're taking our public water, using it, contaminating it with their wastes, and dumping it back into our public lakes and rivers."

He doodled a fox head absentmindedly on the back of the business card I'd given him. "Oh, maybe I trespass a little, and cost those people a bit of time and effort to unplug their pipes when I stuff them up—but they're the ones who're breaking the law. They're committing ecological murder!"

And then his eyes were twinkling again. "When you bring home to a plant owner just what he's doing—when you dump some of his own plants effluent on his office carpet, or toss a dead skunk on the roof of his home—you start getting through to him."

Citizens Take Up the Fox's Battles

The deeds of the Fox have become legend. Once, dressed as a workman, he climbed an industrial chimney that spouted noxious fumes. He measured it, and went home to make a chimney cap. The next night he returned to cap the stack.

Five times he plugged a pipe that poured chemicals into a stream. When the company welded a metal screen over the end, he wriggled in through a manhole and crawled a quarter of a mile to plug the pipe from the inside.

The local police and the guards at plants he's visited would like to catch him. At this writing, he's still at liberty. Have his midnight attacks brought results?

One Aurora plant, after seven raids, has installed an efficient treatment system for its effluent. Citizens groups in the area have been spurred to begin legal battles against other companies. Aurora residents drop their litter into barrels marked with the Fox's insignia.

Though it was those midnight raids that made the news, most of his ecological projects today are lawful ones, carried out with the help of trusted lieutenants by schools and Scout troops. Corporate officials wince at bad publicity, regardless of its source, and more and more concerned citizens are generating headlines.

What Do You Think? _____

1. How might someone opposed to the Fox's actions describe him?
2. Why do you suppose the police want to catch the Fox so badly?
3. Some people consider the Fox a hero; others a villain. How would you describe him? Why?

---

11. Be a Good Samaritan*

Bess Myerson, once Commissioner of Consumer Affairs for New York City, argues that neighborliness and caring for one another are not out of style.

"Whatever happened to neighbors?" It's a good question, and when we find the answer we also may resolve two other troublesome questions of our time: "What's happening to our cities?" "What is our country coming to?"

Each of us, inescapably, is one two-hundred-millionth of the answers.

Whatever happens to us as neighbors, or whatever we permit to happen, is what happens to our cities and our nation eventually. It all begins with the way we live with each other on our own streets, in our big cities and in our small towns, in our farm country and in our suburbs.

I am fortunate in having been able to travel throughout our country and

*Bess Myerson, "Do It Now." Reprinted from *Redbook Magazine,* November 1973. Copyright ' 1973 by The Redbook Publishing Company.

most of the world, but in many ways I've never left the New York neighborhood in which I grew up, the Bronx. The roots of whatever compassion and understanding I may possess are in that old neighborhood, and its people were my teachers.

Mrs. Davis, whose family lived two houses down the street, was one of the people who taught me that good neighbors never turn their backs on trouble. I must have been no more than six years old when I saw strangers carrying furniture out of one apartment onto the street. Along with other youngsters, I watched what for us could be only an "entertainment" to fill our lazy summer afternoon.

We watched the mother and the three children of the family standing quietly as the furniture was piled on the sidewalk. We listened as one of the workmen kept explaining to no one in particular: "We got our orders." We exchanged notes on how much the chairs and beds and tables looked like the furniture in our own houses, and we wondered what terrible thing the family had done to be punished this way.

Then Mrs. Davis lumbered out of her building. Lumbered is the right word. Mrs. Davis was very fat. She not only shook when she walked; just standing still and breathing was enough to keep her in perpetual motion. And when she laughed there was even more bounce to the ounce. She always made us laugh too, and feel better. But she wasn't laughing this time.

"Cossacks!" she shouted at the workmen. "Is this a way to make a living? And where is she supposed to sleep tonight? And how can she make a meal for the family if she's out here and her kitchen is in there?"

By this time she had been joined by other neighbors, all demanding answers to the same basic questions, the only difference being in the names they called the workmen. Mrs. Reardon called them "Black and Tans." Mrs. Scarpi called them "Fascisti." The Roth sisters had a difference of opinion; one called them "Bolsheviks" and the other labeled them "plutocrats."

"I'm not a Cossack," the head furniture carrier said, "or a fascist or a Bolshevik or a plutocrat—and I fought the Black and Tans. Please, ladies, get out of the way. I'm only following orders."

"I order you to take that furniture back," Mrs. Davis shouted. But the law was stronger than Mrs. Davis' order, and the eviction was finished quickly. It wasn't the last one we were to see. Those were the years that some people today like to look back on with amused nostalgia, but that is a view possible only for those who never suffered through them. That was the period called the Depression, and in my neighborhood it took up residence with a long lease.

Mrs. Davis took the evicted family into her own three-room apartment. Others opened their doors in the difficult times that followed. Incidentally, the women never remained angry at the workmen because underneath the shouting and frustration they knew that the workmen might also be one pay check away from a similar fate. Usually an eviction ended with someone's bringing them a cold drink, with mutual cursing about the troubles that follow poor people around and with the workmen chipping in a few dollars for the evicted family.

That was the lesson I was to continue to learn—from my parents, from Mrs. Davis, from Mrs. Reardon, from Mrs. Scarpi, with rare unanimity from the Roth sisters, and from all the people on that street who knew that survival is never a selfish experience. They reached out to one another whenever one was touched by misfortune—an eviction, an illness, an opportunity denied, a way lost. There were no papers to fill out, no lines to wait in; there was no barrier of false pride or indifference between those who needed help at a troubled moment of their lives and those who at that moment had it to give. They lived through it because they helped one another to live.

And it wasn't happening in my neighborhood alone—it was happening in a nation of neighborhoods. People with lifetimes of problems of their own still found time for neighbors whose immediate problems couldn't wait. And if anyone tried to call attention to those countless occasions when they went out of their way to make somebody else's way a little easier, they'd shrug their shoulders and say: "Listen, what's a neighbor for?"

On the Upper West Side of New York City there was an epidemic of muggings that had terrorized the neighborhood. People came out of their homes only when it was absolutely necessary—to get to work or to go to church or run short errands. The muggers were bold because even if they were seen by other residents, there was such an atmosphere of terror that the witnesses hurried past, never interfering, not even calling the police, for fear of retaliation. The list of victims grew, especially among those least able to defend themselves—the elderly, both men and women.

One neighbor, a young man, watched from his window one afternoon, his day off, as the muggers, almost like a victory parade, dominated the empty street. He saw an old man approaching, followed by two muggers. "Somebody ought to do something about those creeps," he said—but in his fear, of course, he meant somebody else. The old man came nearer, the muggers swaggered in for the kill—and in these times, in too many neighborhoods, that's more than a figure of speech.

"Somebody ought to do something," the young man repeated.

"Don't get involved," his wife said.

"You're right," the husband agreed. "They could come after you and the kids when I'm not here—but. . . ." Beautiful word, "but," used in the right place. He was out of the house, swinging at the muggers, too angry to notice the knife slash across his jacket—and then the muggers were gone, the old man was gone and the young man went back into his house. The street seemed the same as before.

But not quite. Newsmen heard about the incident and it was reported in the morning papers. It started something. For three straight days the incident was repeated—different muggers, different neighbors, young and old.

The movement spread. In another part of the city an angry crowd of 50 people chased a mugger right to the doors of the local police precinct house. On Broadway a crowd stood in front of a holdup man's getaway car and kept him pinned inside until the police came. And some other neighborhoods, following the example of resistance, began meetings to plan regular patrols and assistance teams to escort neighbors to and from subway stations, to doctors' appointments, to church and on shopping trips. The Police Auxiliary Squads —civilian assistants—began to receive more applications. Neighborhoods are beginning to look like neighborhoods again instead of muggerhoods.

The muggers are still prowling, of course, but the presence of the neighbors in their own streets, lending strength to one another, has begun to reduce the fear, and that's the beginning of other steps that have been too long in the taking.

A group of young housewives on the Upper East Side of New York City banded together to work for environmental improvement in their own and surrounding neighborhoods. They started cleanup programs, monitored the garbage and trash pickups, started tree-planting programs, printed information about the effect on the environment of various products, began their own newspaper on pollution and consumer problems—and their success inspired other groups in other neighborhoods and in more than a dozen cities across the country.

It's worked wonders for the social environment too. "You know something?" the president of the group said. "We started with six women and now there are forty-five—forty-five women from families who hardly said hello to each other before this or even cared what the family next door was doing. Now we're doing something together; it's easier to care."

A Boy Scout troop in New York City's Borough of Queens had a choice of projects—an overnight camping trip, a boat trip up the Hudson or attendance at a major league ball game. Unanimously, they chose another—one that might not have given them as much personal pleasure (although I'm not sure about that) but one that certainly had a positive impact on many lives beyond their own. They gave a weekend of their time to cleaning unsightly graffiti from the windows and sides of several subway cars, scrawls that have become a growing eyesore suffered with irritation by adult riders, whose most active response has been a mumbled oath about "those kids." Well, some of "those kids" in the Boy Scouts cleaned up some of those cars, maybe closed the generation gap a little and polished another area of the dulling pride of people in their city. How's that for a good deed?

Understanding is a great need where fear exists, and when it is missing, its lack can only add to the loneliness that is the enemy of many in the crowd of the city. Neighbors are those who try to understand. A Brooklyn youth club made regular weekly visits to an old-age center a few blocks from their church. They read to the elderly residents, they found topics to share, they listened to one another, they enjoyed one another. The boys and girls are Black; the elderly men and women are Jewish. Color lines and religious differences and generation gaps don't stand a chance against human effort, and neighborhoods don't stand a chance without it.

There's a neighborhood that's on a tightrope, balancing between remaining livable and falling into chaos. The residents try hard to keep up the old **103** houses, keep down the street crime and keep the younger kids in line. But there is one enemy that was beginning to be too much for them: dope. The neighborhood was becoming a gathering point for addicts who threatened passers-by, lured younger kids into their orbit to nowhere, broke into apartments to steal anything they could carry, made sleep impossible most of the night with their street noise and threatened to destroy whatever community-improvement projects the residents had started.

Something had to be done—immediately—without waiting for sociological surveys or political programs to catch up to the danger, and the "funding" of the effort would have to be drawn from the neighbors' own initiative and energy. A group of mothers organized a telephone brigade, with about 20 members who lived in various locations throughout the neighborhood who could monitor every street corner and almost every doorway by looking through their own apartment windows. When they saw a dope pusher or addict heading for trouble, they called the right numbers to report the problem and kept calling until the right people came to take the problem off the streets of their neighborhood and put them into treatment.

"Some of the kids call us squealers," one mother said after reporting a loud and abusive crowd that her own seemed on the verge of joining, "but I damn sure would rather be this kind of squealer than the mother of a dead son."

These are all comparatively small steps in the larger scheme of reclaiming our neighborhoods and helping neighbors find one another again, but I've written about them because I shared them and because they are down-to-earth examples of how each and all of us can add our individual efforts to the already existing opportunities for neighborhood participation. They're the extra commitments that help us to find not only the best in each other but also the best in ourselves. And the best has always been good enough for any generation of neighborhoods in our nation of neighborhoods, and anything less than the best begins on our own doorsteps.

Most of us know the truth of that. So let's open our doors—Mrs. Davis may be out there. In fact, you may be Mrs. Davis and you may find yourself back in your old neighborhood.

What Do You Think? _____

1. Should people be good neighbors and "get involved"? Why or why not?
2. If people cared for and watched over one another more, do you think crime, vandalism, and conflict would decrease?
3. How do people go about changing—go about learning to care again—to practice good samaritanism?

12. Fight Back*

Here is a viewpoint that violence, under certain conditions and in certain circumstances, is justified.

There is this scene in the movie *Elmer Gantry* which was adapted from the Sinclair Lewis novel of the same title, in which this thug is slapping this prostitute around. At which point Burt Lancaster comes in, walks over to the thug and says something like, "Hey, fellow, don't you know that hurts?" And smashes his fist magnificently up against the thug's head and generally kicks the thug around, just to emphasize the point.

It was a beautiful moment in the movie, and it crystallized my own attitude toward the merits (moral and practical) of nonviolence as a policy for Negroes. The perpetrators of violence must be made to know how it feels to be recipients of violence. How can they know unless we teach them?

I remember as a child on Virgin Street in Macon, Ga., there was this boy who took delight in punching me, and one of his favorite sports was twisting my arm. Onlookers would try to prevail upon him: "Shame! Shame! The Lord is not going to bless you!" Which admonitions seemed to spur my adversary on and on.

One day, I put two "alley apples" (pieces of brick) in my trousers' pockets and ventured forth. I was hardly out in the sun-washed streets before bully boy playfully accosted me. He immediately began his game of punching me in the stomach, laughing all the while. He was almost a foot taller than I, but I reached into my pockets and leaped up at both sides of his head with the alley apples. Bully boy ran off. We later became great friends. We never could have become friends on the basis of him kicking my backside and my counter-attack consisting solely of "Peace, brother!"

The one thing most friends and all enemies of the Afro-American have agreed upon is that we are ordained by nature and by God to be nonviolent. And so a new myth about the Negro is abroad throughout the land, to go with the old myths of laziness and rhythm and irresponsibility and sexual prowess. In the last third of the 20th century, when the disfranchised all over the earth are on the move, the world is being told that the good old U.S.A. has evolved a new type of *Homo sapiens,* the nonviolent Negro. The most disturbing aspect of this question is that many Negroes have bought this myth and are spreading it around.

One of the basic attributes of manhood (when we say manhood, we mean

*Excerpted from John Oliver Killens, *Black Man's Burden.* Copyright © 1965 by John Oliver Killens. Reprinted by permission of Trident Press, a division of Simon & Schuster, Inc. **105**

womanhood, selfhood) is the right of self-defense. In the psychological castration of the Negro, the denial of his right of self-defense has been one of the main instruments. Let me make one thing clear: I am not at the moment interested in the question of the so-called castration of the American male by American womanhood, or "Momism." White Moma is a victim too. Indeed. Madame Simone de Beauvoir in *The Second Sex* hit the bull's-eye when she made the analogy between the training of bourgeois girls and the training of American Negroes to know their place and to stay forever in it.

I grew up in Macon under a "separate but equal" public-school system. On our way to our wooden-frame school we black kids had to walk through a middle-class white neighborhood. One day in spring a white boy on the way home from his pretty brick school with his comrades said innocently enough, "Hey, nigger, what you learn in school today?" Friendly-like.

"I learned your mother was a whore," the sassy black boy answered, not in the spirit of nonviolence. We were 7 to 11 years of age.

The black boy's buddies laughed angrily, uproariously. The white lad slapped the black boy's face, and that was how the "race riot" started. We fist-fought, we rock-battled, we used sticks and baseball bats and everything else that came to hand. Nobody won. The "race riot" just sort of petered out. We black kids went home with cut lips and bloody noses, but we went home proud and happy and got our backsides whipped for tearing our school clothes, and by the next morning we had almost forgotten it.

Just before noon the next day our school yard swarmed with policemen. They strode into the classroom without so much as a "good morning" to the teachers and dragged kids out. They took those who had been in the "riot" and some who'd never even heard of it. The next move was to bring scared black mothers to the jailhouses to whip their children in order to "teach them they must not fight white children." Not a single white lad was arrested—naturally. And so they drove the lesson home. The black American must expect his person to be violated by the white man, but he must know that the white man's person is inviolable.

As an African-American, especially in the hospitable Southland, I concede that nonviolence is a legitimate tactic. It is practical and pragmatic; it has placed the question morally before the nation and the world. But the tendency is to take a tactic and build it into a way of life, to construct a whole new ideology and rhetoric around it. The danger is that all other means of struggle will be proscribed.

We black folk must never, tacitly[1] or otherwise, surrender one single right guaranteed to any other American. The right of self-defense is the most basic of human rights, recognized by all people everywhere. It is certainly more important than the right to eat frankfurters while sitting down or to get a black haircut in a white barbershop, or to get a night's lodging in Mrs. Murphy's flophouse, may the Good Lord rest her soul. Indeed, it is more important than

[1]Expressed or carried on without words or speech.

the right to vote. In many places in the South the Negro can't get to the polls without the right of self-defense.

A man's home is his castle, but a man's "castle" is really made of flesh and bones and heart and soul. One's castle is also one's wife and children, one's people, one's dignity. Invade this castle at your peril is the way the freedom script must read.

I was in Montgomery during the bus-protest movement. I was told on more than one occasion that most Negro men had stopped riding the buses long before the protest started because they could not stand to hear their women insulted by the brave bus drivers. Here the alternatives were sharp and clear: debasement, death, or tired feet. Black citizens of Montgomery did not have the right to be violent, by word or action, toward men who practiced every type of violence against them.

I also know that despite all the preaching about nonviolence, the South is an armed camp. It always has been, ever since I can remember. The first time my wife, who is Brooklyn-born, went south with me, she was shocked to see so many guns in African-American homes. Of course, the white establishment has even vaster power, including the guns of the forces of law and order. . . .

Before leading the Negro people of Birmingham into a demonstration in that city, the Rev. Martin Luther King was reported to have said, "If blood is shed, let it be our blood!" But our blood has always been the blood that was shed. And where is the morality that makes the white racist's blood more sacred than that of black children? I cannot believe that Dr. King meant these words, if indeed he ever uttered them. I can only believe that he got carried away by the dramatics of the moment. Dr. King is one of the men whom I hold in great esteem. We have been friends since 1957. But he loses me and millions of other black Americans when he calls upon us to love our abusers.

"Kick me and I will still love you! Spit on me and I will still love you!"

My daughter, who loves him dearly, heard him say words to this effect on the radio one day. She was in tears for her black hero, "Daddy! Daddy! What's the matter with Rev. King? What's the matter with Rev. King?"

I agree with Chuck and Barbara (my son and daughter). There is no dignity for me in allowing a man to spit on me with impunity. There is only sickness on the part of both of us, and it will beget an ever greater sickness. It degrades me and brutalizes him. If black folk were so sick as to love those who practice genocide against us, we would not deserve human consideration.

The advocates of nonviolence have not reckoned with the psychological needs of black America. There is in many Negroes a deep need to practice violence against their white tormentors. We black folk clearly loved the great Joe Louis, the heavyweight champion the white folk dubbed "The Brown Bomber." Each time he whipped another white man, black hearts overflowed with joy. Joe was strong wine for our much-abused egos.

I was at Yankee Stadium the night our champ knocked out Max Schmeling, the German fighter, in the first round. I saw black men who were strangers embrace each other, unashamedly, and weep for joy. And Joe was in the **107**

American tradition. Americans have always been men of violence and proud of it.

We are a country born in violence. Malcolm X, the Black Nationalist leader who was murdered, knew this basic truth. He did not preach violence, but he did advocate self-defense. That is one of the reasons he had such tremendous attraction for the people of the ghetto. What I am saying is that the so-called race riots are healthier (from the point of view of the ghetto people) than the internecine[2] gang warfare which was the vogue in the ghettos a few years ago, when black teen-agers killed each other or killed equally helpless Puerto Ricans, as was often the case in New York City. Historically in the black ghettos the helpless and hopeless have practiced violence on each other. Stand around the emergency entrance at Harlem Hospital of a Saturday night and check the business in black blood drawn by black hands that comes in every weekend.

It is time for Americans (black and white) to stop hoodwinking themselves. Nonviolence is a tactic, but it must never be a way of life for the black American. Just because I love myself, the black Me, why do white Americans (especially liberals) think it means I have to hate the white American You? We black and white folk in the U.S.A. have to settle many things between us before the matter of love can be discussed. For one thing, if you practice violence against me, I mean to give it back to you in kind.

Most black folk believe in the kind of nonviolence that keeps everybody nonviolent. For example: In a certain cotton country in the heart of Dixieland, black folk, most of them sharecroppers, asserted their right to vote and were driven from the land. For several years they lived in tents and of a Saturday evening white pranksters had a playful way of driving out to Tent City and shooting into it. A couple of campers were injured, including a pregnant woman. Complaints to the authorities got no results at all. So one Saturday evening, when the pranksters turned up just to have a little sport, the campers (lacking a sense of humor) returned the fire. A young relative of the sheriff got his arm shattered. The sheriff got out there in a hurry and found rifles shining out of every tent. He sent for the Negro leader.

"Tell them to give up them rifles, boy. I can't protect 'em less'n they surrender up them rifles."

Whereupon the 35-year-old "boy" said, "We figured you was kind of busy, Sheriff. We thought we'd give you a helping hand and protect our own selves." There was no more racial violence in the county for a long time.

Let us speak plainly to each other. Your black brother is spoiling for a fight in affirmation of his selfhood. This is the meaning of Watts and Harlem and Bedford-Stuyvesant. It seems to me, you folk who abhor violence, you are barking up the wrong tree when you come to black folk and call on them to

[2]Of or involving conflict within a group.

be nonviolent. Go to the attackers. Go to the ones who start the fire, not to the firefighters. Insist that your Government place the same premium on black life as it does on white. As far as I can ascertain, no white American has ever been condemned to death by the courts for taking a black life.

The Deacons of Defense, the Negro self-defense organization that started in Louisiana not long ago, is going to mushroom and increasingly become a necessary appendage to the civil-rights movement. This should be welcomed by everyone who is sincere about the "Negro revolution." It accomplishes three things simultaneously. It makes certain that the Government will play the role of the fire department, the pacifier. Second: The actual physical presence of the Deacons (or any similar group) will go a long way in staying the hands of the violence makers. Third: It further affirms the black Americans' determination to exercise every right enjoyed by all other Americans.

Otherwise we're in for longer and hotter summers. There are all kinds among us black folks. Gentle ones and angry ones, forgiving and vindictive, and every single one is determined to be free. Julian Bond, poet, SNCC leader and duly elected member of the Georgia legislature (his seat was denied him because of his pronouncements on Vietnam), summed up the situation when he wrote:

> "Look at that gal shake that thing.
> We cannot all be Martin Luther King."

I believe he meant, among other things, that whites cannot expect Negroes to be different—that is, more saintly than whites are—and that most black folk are in no mood to give up the right to defend themselves.

What Do You Think? _____

1. The author of this article is addressing himself primarily to the case of black people in America. Would it apply to whites as well?
2. Is violence ever justified? If so, when? If not, why not? Explain your reasoning.

---

13. Don't Worry*

Many people do not view the political system as related to violence. Others regard politics as the heart of American life and thus an influence on all behavior. In an

*Excerpted from Nelson W. Polsky and Aaron B. Wildavsky, *Presidential Elections*. New York: Charles Scribner's Sons, 1964.

Among the most important things accomplished by a political system like ours is that it rules out the most extreme alternatives. Knowing that policies which would outrage significant groups in the country would result in a stream of protest leading to loss of the next election, the party in power is restrained from the worst excesses. For people in countries like America or Great Britain, this may be difficult to appreciate precisely because they rarely have occasion to witness these extremes; extreme policies are effectively ruled out by the party system and free elections. This is not so everywhere and we can get an insight into what is possible when the ultimate restraint of free elections is missing. Imagine that in 1956 the United States repudiated its national debt on the ground that it was inflationary. Suppose that ten years previously our government had confiscated about nine-tenths of all savings by issuing new currency worth only a tenth of the old. No doubt there would have been riots in the streets, petitions galore, furious political participation by millions of formerly inactive citizens, and a complete change of government as soon as the election laws allowed. Can we conceive of a situation in which our government would ship millions of tons of wheat abroad while millions of our own people were starving? All these extreme policies have been pursued by the Soviet Union, and food exports from China continue today though its people are living barely at the subsistence level. We are more fortunate than we know if we can say that it is difficult or impossible to imagine extreme policies like these being carried out. Indeed, it is hard to imagine that anyone in a responsible position would think of such policies, let alone attempt to promulgate[1] them. Here we come to a key point. No one thinks about these things seriously because everyone understands that they simply could not be done.

Extreme policies are ruled out in a more subtle way; free elections discourage persons with extreme views from running for office because possible allies of such people know that they cannot win and that, if they do, their victories will last only until the next election. Extremists deprive too many people of too many of their preferred policies to win office easily. Thus we find that would-be Presidential aspirants do not get far if they are known publicly to hold bigoted views about racial or religious minorities or if they have done or said things which suggest that they are extremely hostile to large population groups such as laborers or small businessmen. Moreover, those who do attain office and wish to enjoy its benefits find that compromise and conciliation bring greater rewards than hostility and intransigence.[2] The political system conditions those who accept the rules of free elections to moderate behavior.

[1]Make known by open declaration.

[2]The state of refusing to compromise.

Is a ballot a real alternative to the bullet? Why or why not?

---

14. In Defense of Violence*

Lastly, the view that violence may be useful and justified under special circumstances. The article below presents some opinions of clerics and churchmen in favor of violent action. Is this a paradox?

At the heart of the Christian message is peace on earth, good will to men. In spite of this injunction to concord and reconciliation, a growing number of theologians and churchmen are willing to endorse violence and even revolution as a means of achieving social justice. In Detroit last October, at a conference on Church and Society sponsored by the National Council of Churches, one group of delegates argued that Christians should accept violence as a valid means of attacking the problems of racism and poverty. A proposal that will be debated at the World Council of Churches' Fourth Assembly in Sweden this July declares that "there are situations in which revolutionary action to achieve a radical change of the political regime seems the only way to arrive at a social order based on justice."

Christian enthusiasm for revolution is probably strongest in Latin America where Camilo Torres, a Colombian priest who was killed in a skirmish after he turned guerrilla, has become something of an uncanonized saint to many young Roman Catholics. Last summer, 17 Latin American bishops issued a commentary on Pope Paul's encyclical Populorum Progressio, warning that revolution might well prove to be the only way of removing the continent's economic and social inequities. "Misery caused by man unto man," says Father Paul Charbonneau, a Belgian-born priest who serves in Sao Paulo, "is the form of violence in itself, varying only in degree and extension from armed violence." . . .

Some churchmen contend that a theology of violence applies with equal validity to the U.S., because of the manifest despair and poverty of the Negro ghetto. Ralph Potter of the Harvard Divinity School says that the new debate over violence is based on "the perception that justice may reside with those who have been voiceless before." The Rev. William Cook, a Methodist minister with the interfaith council on Religion and International Affairs, thinks

*Excerpted from "In Defense of Violence," *Time,* March 15, 1968. Reprinted by permission from TIME, The Weekly Newsmagazine, copyright © Time, Inc., 1968.

that last year's Newark and Detroit riots "were not only understandable but justifiable."

Theologians who condone violence can quote Scripture to back their cause. Ignoring St. Paul's injunction in Romans to "let every person be subject to the governing authorities," they cite the example of the Old Testament prophets who urged Israel to rebel against tyrants, Christ's violent action in chasing the money-changers from the Temple. Both Catholic and Protestant theologians of violence argue that their thinking is nothing more than an extension of the just-war doctrine, which, in brief, says that a war is moral when a good cause is at stake, or when a nation is unfairly attacked. Father Riga argues that the existence of social injustice within a country can be as much of an evil as an enemy at the gate, and thus a violent revolution may be the only way to eradicate it.

What Do You Think? _____

1. Is a war "moral" when a just cause is at stake?
2. Might some people be surprised that ministers and priests may be among those who advocate violence? Why or why not?

ACTIVITIES FOR INVOLVEMENT

1. Make up your own definition of force. Of coercion. Compare these with the idea of violence you developed as you read this book. Look up definitions of these words in the dictionary. Compare them to your own definitions. In what ways are the definitions of violence, force, and coercion similar? Different? How would you explain these similarities and differences?

2. Explain why you would agree or disagree with each of the following definitions of violence:
   a. Any act whereby a person's mind or body is damaged, either physically or psychologically
   b. All harm done to man, animal, or ecology
   c. Only physical damage to a person or animal
   d. Force used for destructive purposes
   e. Whenever someone is forced to act contrary to his or her wishes

3. Is all manner of violence equally destructive? Rate the examples below on a scale from 0 to 5; 0 for nonviolence, 1 for small-scale violence, on up to 5 for extreme violence.
   a. An old man, slightly drunken, and wearing dirty, torn clothes, is walking down the street. Several children are dancing around and

yelling at him. They call him a "bum," "rag-man," "sot," "boozer," and other such names.

b. Thousands of prisoners revolt and take over a prison. They take many hostages, from guards to visitors. When asked, they refuse to give up to authorities. The police attack the prison, killing hostages and prisoners alike. The toll is 100 wounded and 40 dead. No guns are found on the prisoners.

c. Three boys kidnap a boy they do not like. They take him to a secluded place in a park and proceed to torture him. After they cut and burn him, he pleads on his knees to be released. Finally, they let him go home.

d. Political protesters march through a public park. They are jostled by crowds who have turned out to watch. The marchers trample all the grass in sight and leave handbills all over the area. At the end of the demonstration, the park is worn and covered with garbage.

e. A man is spotted trying to jump off a building. As he is about to leap, three bystanders run over to him and restrain him. The man cries and complains bitterly that he does not want to be saved, but they hold him anyway until the police come and take him away.

f. An elderly lady is walking down the path to her doorway. As she approaches the door, a young man darts out of a nearby bush and grabs her purse. She screams and he runs down the alley and disappears.

g. A mentally ill man hides in the tower of a tall building and begins shooting at people in the street. The sniper kills 11 people before he is stopped.

h. An Indian tribe opposed to the takeover of its lands by the government is attacked without notice. Soldiers burn the Indians' homes and kill as many members of the tribe as they can find—men, women, and children. Only 20 out of 500 survive.

4. Write down all of the examples of violence that you personally witness in a week of your life. Check those you think were most serious. Compare your compilation with those of several of your friends. What differences do you notice? Try to reach an agreed-on definition of violence at this point.

5. Do a research paper in which you select four historical periods, each 10 years in length. One period should be the decade 1960–1970, while the other periods might be chosen from late eighteenth, late nineteenth, or early twentieth century America. Collect historical and news sources about the violence in each period, focusing on riots, rebellions, strikes, and lynchings. Keep count of each type of violence. Rate each example on a scale of 1 to 5, based on increasing intensity. Make a chart comparing each

period. In which time period was there the greatest number of examples? The most violent? Is our own time period more, or less, violent than past ones? Has the intensity decreased or increased over the years?

6. Invite a lawyer to discuss the legal definitions of force, coercion, and violence with the class. Compare the legal idea of violence with your own; with the dictionary's. Who has the stricter definition? The loosest? Why is this? See if you can find a statement or article describing the legal conceptions of violence, force, and coercion in another country. Compare these definitions with the others you have formulated or obtained.

7. Write to the Gallup and Harris polling organizations for past studies of people's feelings about crimes, social protest, gun laws, and intergroup conflict. Make a chart comparing how people feel now with how they felt in the middle and late 1960s. Are people more optimistic or more pessimistic about the amount of violence exhibited in American life? Are they more fearful or less so? How do you feel?

8. Some people believe that violence should be viewed as a very broad concept, which includes psychological harm. Join with several of your classmates and draw up a list of cases that you think are examples of psychological violence. How would your list compare with this list? Who has committed the violence in each of the following examples?

   a. A very frail elderly woman is sent against her wishes to a home for the aged. There she loses all interest in doing anything and soon passes away. Have her children done violence to her? Has she done it to herself? Is the home responsible?

   b. A young boy of 12 is pushed by his parents to always be the best in sports, schoolwork, everything. He works very hard and generally succeeds. Yet, a few failures cause intense depression and he commits suicide. Who has been violent in this situation and to whom?

   c. At a party, several teenagers drop LSD into one of their friend's drinks—just for laughs. He goes wild and winds up in the hospital for a few days—but survives. Has he been the victim of violence or only a prank?

   d. A husband who is very nervous about succeeding at his job is constantly criticized by his wife and relatives about his lack of success. Slowly, he develops a very bad ulcer and is finally hospitalized. Has violence played a part in this case?

   e. A public inquiry by a state commission reveals that mental patients are being given neglectful and indifferent care and left in filthy conditions in several state hospitals. They are often cheated out of allowance checks and allowed to wander the grounds ragged and hungry. Has violence been done to these people by the hospital staff? Only by its leadership? Or by society's indifference? (How would you feel about this one if the study showed the poor care and facilities were largely due to a lack of money from state sources?)

f. A very sick child who has been ill for many years has been hovering on the edge of death for days. The child is suffering great pain and there is no known cure. In great anguish, the parents order the doctor to cease treatment and the doctor complies. The child dies a day later. Is this violence? By the parents? The doctor? By causes over which human beings have no control?

BIBLIOGRAPHY
For Further Study

BOOKS

BACH, GEORGE, and HERBERT GOLDBERG • *Creative Aggression.* • Garden City, N.Y.: Doubleday & Company, 1974.

BAKER, MARILYN, with SALLY BROMPTON • *The Inside Story of Patricia Hearst and the S.L.A.* • New York: Macmillan Company, 1974.

BROEHL, WAYNE, JR. • *The Molly Maguires* • Cambridge, Mass.: Harvard University Press, 1964.

BUGLIOSI, VINCENT • *Helter Skelter: The True Story of the Manson Murders* • New York: W. W. Norton & Company, 1974.

CAUGHEY, JOHN (ed.) • *Their Majesties the Mob* • Chicago: University of Chicago Press, 1960.

CHALMERS, DAVID M. • *Hooded Americanism* • Garden City, N.Y.: Doubleday & Company, 1965.

CLINE, VICTOR B. • *Where Do You Draw the Line: An Exploration into Media Violence, Pornography, and Censorship* • Brigham Young University Press, 1974.

CROOK, WILLIAM H., and ROSS THOMAS • *Warriors for the Poor: The Story of Vista* • New York: William Morrow & Co., 1969.

DALEY, CHARLES U. • *Urban Violence* • Chicago: University of Chicago Press, 1969.

DOLLARD, JOHN, et al. • *Frustration and Aggression* • New Haven, Conn.: Yale University Press, 1939.

ENDELMAN, SHALOM (ed.) • *Violence in the Streets* • Chicago: Quadrangle Books, 1968.

FOREMAN, JAMES • *Law and Disorder* • Camden, N.J.: Nelson & Sons, 1972.

FROMM, ERICH • *The Anatomy of Human Destructiveness* • New York: Holt, Rinehart & Winston, 1973.

GREY, ZANE • *To the Last Man* • New York: Harper & Row, 1922.

GUNN, JOHN • *Violence* • New York: Praeger, 1973.

GURR, TED ROBERT • *Why Men Rebel* • Princeton, N.J.: Princeton University Press, 1970.

HEAPS, WILLARD A. • *Riots, U.S.A.: 1765–1970,* rev. ed. • New York: Seabury Press, 1970.

HOLLEN, EUGENE • *Frontier Violence: Another Look* • New York: Oxford University Press, 1974.

HORAN, JAMES D. • *The Pinkertons: The Detective Dynasty that Made History* • New York: Crown Press, 1968.

JONES, VIRGIL CARRINGTON • *The Hatfields and the McCoys* • Chapel Hill, N.C.: University of North Carolina Press, 1948.

LISTON, ROBERT • *Violence in America* • New York: Julian Messner, 1974.

MADISON, ARNOLD • *Vandalism* • New York: Seabury Press, 1970.

MADISON, ARNOLD • *Vigilantism in America* • New York: Seabury Press, 1973.

OLSEN, JACK • *The Man with the Candy: The Story of the Houston Mass Murders* • New York: Simon & Schuster, 1974.

RAY, JO ANNE • *American Assassins* • Lerner, 1974.

REYNOLDS, FRANK • *Freewheelin' Frank: Secretary of the Angels* • New York: Grove Press, 1967.

RUBENSTEIN, RICHARD E. • *Rebels in Eden* • Boston: Little, Brown and Company, 1970.

RUDE, GEORGE • *The Crowd in History* • New York: John Wiley & Sons, 1964.

SULLIVAN, LEON, and MacRAE SMITH • *Build, Brother, Build* • 1969.

WASKOW, ARTHUR I. • *From Race Riot to Sit-In* • Garden City, N.Y.: Doubleday and Company, 1966.

PAPERBACK BOOKS

BERGER, THOMAS • *Little Big Man* • New York: Simon & Schuster, 1970.

BRALY, MALCOLM • *On the Yard* • Greenwich, Conn.: Fawcett World (Premier), 1971.

BRINTON, CRANE • *The Anatomy of Revolution* • New York: Vintage Books, 1955.

CAPOTE, TRUMAN • *In Cold Blood* • New York: Signet Books, 1968.

CLARK, RAMSEY • *Crime in America* • New York: Pocket Books, 1971.

CLARK, WALTER VAN TILBURG • *The Ox-Bow Incident* • New York: Signet Books-New American Library, 1940.

CONOT, ROBERT • *Rivers of Blood, Years of Darkness* • New York: Bantam Books, 1967.

CRISTINA, FRANK, and TERESA CRISTINA • *Billy Jack* • New York: Avon, 1973.

FANON, FRANTZ • *The Wretched of the Earth* • New York: Grove Press, 1968.

GADDIS, THOMAS E., and JAMES O. LONG • *Killer: A Journal of Murder* • Greenwich, Conn.: Fawcett World (Premier), 1970.

HENRY, A. F., and J. F. SHORT, JR. • *Suicide and Homicide* • New York: Free Press.

IRWIN, THEODORE • *To Combat Child Abuse and Neglect* • Washington, D.C.: Public Affairs Committee pamphlet No. 508, 1974.

KOZOL, JONATHAN • *Death at an Early Age* • Boston: Houghton-Mifflin Co., 1967.

LARSEN, OTTO (ed.) • *Violence and the Mass Media* • New York: Harper & Row, 1968.

LENS, SIDNEY • *Radicalism in America* • New York: Thomas Y. Crowell Co., 1969.

LORENZ, CONRAD • *On Aggression* • New York: Bantam Books, 1966.

LYND, STAUGHTON (ed.) • *Nonviolence in America: A Documentary History* • Indianapolis, Ind.: Bobbs-Merrill Co., 1966.

MAAS, PETER • *Serpico* • New York: Bantam Books, 1974.

MAAS, PETER • *The Valachi Papers* • New York: Bantam Books, 1964.

McKAY, BIDGE • *Training for Nonviolent Action for High School Students* • Friends Peace Committee, 1971.

STYRON, WILLIAM • *The Confessions of Nat Turner* • New York: Signet Books—New American Library, 1968.

SUTHERLAND, E. H. • *The Professional Thief* • Chicago: Phoenix Books, 1937.
THOMPSON, THOMAS • *Richie* • New York: Bantam Books, 1974.
WHITTEMORE, L. H. • *The Super Cops* • New York: Bantam Books, 1973.
WHYTE, WILLIAM FOOTE • *Street Corner Society: The Social Structure of an Italian Slum* • Chicago: Phoenix Books (University of Chicago Press), 1955.

REPORTS

The Challenge of Crime in a Free Society: A Report of the President's Commission on Law Enforcement and Administration of Justice • Washington, D.C.: U.S. Government Printing Office, 1967.

Crime in the U.S.: Uniform Crime Reports—1972, by the Federal Bureau of Investigation • Washington, D.C.: Supt. of Documents, Order No. J/14/1972.

The Politics of Protest: Violent Aspects of Protest and Confrontation, a staff report to the National Commission on the Causes and Prevention of Violence prepared by Jerome Skolwick et al. • Washington, D.C.: U.S. Government Printing Office, 1969.

Report of the National Advisory Commission on Civil Disorders • New York: Bantam Books, 1968.

The Reports of the President's Commission on Campus Unrest • New York: Avon Books, 1971.

Rights in Conflict, a report submitted to the National Commission on the Causes and Prevention of Violence by Daniel Walker • New York: National American Library, 1968.

Struggle for Justice: A Report on Crime and Punishment in America, by American Friends Service Committee • New York: Hill & Wang, 1971.

Violence in America: Historical and Comparative Perspectives, a report to the National Commission on the Causes and Prevention of Violence • June 1969.

ARTICLES

"Agnew's Talk with Five Students" • *U.S. News & World Report,* October 12, 1970.
ARNOLD, O. C. • "Fight Fiercely Christians" • *Christian Century,* June 19, 1968.
BEHRMAN, I. • "Understanding Man's Aggressiveness" • *UNESCO Courier,* August 1970.
BETTELHEIM, BRUNO • "Children Must Learn to Fear" • *The New York Times Magazine, April 13, 1969.*
BOTWIN, C. • "Violence and the City Child" • *The New York Times Magazine,* January 11, 1970.
"Citizen's War on Crime" • *U.S. News & World Report,* March 23, 1970.
GARDNER, JOHN • "Plain Talk About Hatred and Violence" • *Reader's Digest,* June 1968.
GARVER, NEWTON • "What Violence Is" • *The Nation,* June 24, 1968.
GORER, GEOFFREY • "Man Has No 'Killer' Instinct" • *The New York Times Magazine,* November 17, 1966.
HART, JEFFREY • "Violence in America" • *National Review,* June 18, 1968.
HART, JOHN • "Coming Revolution in America" • *National Review,* July 2, 1968.
KUHN, H. B. • "Theology of Violence?" • *Christianity Today,* November 22, 1968.
MENNINGER, KARL A. • "Psychiatrist Looks at Violence" • *Catholic World,* September 1969.

NELSON, B. • "Exploring the Causes of Urban Riots" • *Science,* July 14, 1968.

POPPY, J. • "Violence: We Can End It" • *Look,* June 10, 1969.

RANLY, E. W. • "Ways of Violence" • *America,* September 12, 1970.

REISS, ALBERT J., JR. • "How Common Is Police Brutality?" • *Trans-action,* July-August 1968.

SCHLESINGER, ARTHUR, JR. • "America, 1968: The Politics of Violence" • *Harper's,* August 1968.

STEWART, T. D. • "Fossil Evidence of Human Violence" • *Trans-action,* May 1969.

TOBIN, R. L. • "More Violent than Ever: Preoccupation with Bad News in the Mass Media" • *Saturday Review,* November 9, 1968.

WOETZEL, R. K. • "Crime and Violence in American Life" • *Current History,* October 1968.

WOLFGANG, MARVIN E. • "Who Kills Whom?" • *Psychology Today,* Vol. 3, No. 5, October 1969.

FILMS

Anatomy of Violence (30 min; B/W; Indiana University Audio-Visual Center) • Discussions and examples of theories behind violence.

Black and White: Unless We Learn to Live Together (15 min; color, American Educational film) • A sensitive film about two men who tried to prevent conflict and hatred.

Black and White Uptight (35 min; color; Avanti Films) • The way in which hate is learned is explored in this film. Background is given to the feelings that eventually develop into riots. Solutions are discussed and the desire for a new attitude indicated.

Civil Disorder: The Kerner Report (two parts, 56 min; B/W, Indiana University Audio-Visual Center) • Documentary based on the famous report *Crime and the Criminal* (33 min; B/W, learning Corporation of America); A study, in depth, of a single criminal—taken from the film version of *In Cold Blood.*

The Coffee House (27 min; B/W; Paulist Productions) • An example of teenage violence.

Comics and Kids (14 min; color; Henk Newhouse/Novo) • A documentary about the kinds of brutal and aggressive scenes kids find in their comic books.

Crime and Delinquency (29 min; B/W; Indiana University Audio-Visual Center) • An introduction to the movement from crime in the early years to full-fledged criminality later in life.

Dead Birds (60 min; color; Contemporary Films) • The perpetual warfare system of New Guinea's highland tribes.

Dead Man Coming (24 min; B/W, Pyramid Films) • Prison life and what it is like afterward for an ex-convict.

The Face of Crime (52 min; B/W; CBS News) • A two-part documentary report on new methods of prisoner treatment. Social and psychological features are stressed in rehabilitation rather than punishment.

"I Have a Dream . . .": The Life of Martin Luther King (35 min; B/W; CBS News) • The film brings a better understanding of the philosophies and ideals that Martin Luther King exemplified. In telling the story of Dr. King, nonviolence is practiced as a part of the civil rights movements.

The Invincible Weapon (27 min; B/W; Paulist Productions) • Self-destruction and suicide as examples of violent behavior toward the self.

The Jail (80 min; B/W; Cinema 5) • A raw view of life in prison.

Joshua (15 min; B/W; AC I films) • Psychological study of some of the drives basic to human conflict on the personal level.

Law and Order Versus Dissent (10 min; B/W; Henk Newhouse/Novo) • A documentary raising questions about the legal and social aspects of dissent.

Man in the Middle (27 min; B/W; Paulist Productions) • An example of racial hostility and conflict.

Metropolis: Creator or Destroyer? (29 min; B/W; Indiana University Audio-Visual Center) • A review of the advantages and disadvantages of the urban way of life.

Play It Cool: A Question of Control (15 min; color; CCM Films) • Police behavior as a stimulant to violence, or as a controlling force in lessening conflict. A discussion of police attitudes and how they influence people's behavior.

The Question of Violence (59 min; B/W; Indiana University Audio-Visual Center) • An overview of violence in America; a broad and many-faceted look at conflict throughout the land.

Revolution in Human Expectation (29 min; B/W; Indiana University Audio-Visual Center) • Poverty as a springboard to revolt and dissatisfaction with one's position in society.

Run! (16 min; B/W produced and directed by Jack Kuper) • An allegory of the destructiveness of high-pressure society. A man tries to counter these pressures by turning to drugs, but finally fails.

Social Confrontation: The Battle of Michigan Avenue (10 min; B/W; Henk Newhouse/-Novo) • A documentary of the riots between police and demonstrators during the 1968 Democratic National Convention in Chicago.

Time of the Locust (12 min; B/W; produced and directed by Peter Gessner) • An antiwar film made from Vietnam footage. Rather disturbing in its execution and sympathetic of the victims of war.

Violence and Vandalism (15 min; color; American Educational Films) • Wanton destruction, portrayed and probed.

MULTIMEDIA

1877—The Great Strike (two filmstrips, two long-playing records/cassettes and Teacher's Guide, Multi-Media Productions, 1973). A case study of labor-management conflict.

John Brown (one filmstrip, one record/cassette, and Teacher's Guide, Multi-Media Productions, 1973). A famous historical example of violence used against evil.

Violence in Society (two filmstrips, two long-playing records/cassettes and Teacher's Guide, Multi-Media Productions, 1973). Wide-ranging discussion with special attention to gun control.

DATE DUE

MAY 2 1979			
NOV 2 6 1980			
APR 2 7			
OCT 16 1986			
OCT 28 1986			
NOV 11 1986			
DEC 0 1 1986			
DEC 0 1 1986			
APR 2 0 1987			
MAY 0 4 1987			

30 505 JOSTEN'S